PROMISE KIDS ON THE PROMISE PATH

Developed by Scottie May
Written by Cindy Kenney
Critter County Stories by Paula Bussard

Accelerated spiritual growth for your entire congregation

PROMISE KIDS ON THE PROMISE PATH: LEARN-
ING HOW TO FOLLOW GOD'S DIRECTIONS
CHILDREN'S CURRICULUM: GRADES 1–6
Developer: Scottie May
Writer: Cindy Kenney
Critter County Story Writer: Paula Bussard
Songwriters: Ken Goodwin, Roger Cadle,
Christine Wyrtzen
Song Arrangements: Roger Cadle, Bobby Fisher
Editors: Jeanette Dall, Laurie Mains, Marian Oliver
Cover Design: De Leon Design
Text Design: De Leon Design
Cover and Text Illustrations: De Leon Design

© 1999 Mainstay Church Resources
Published by Mainstay Church Resources

Printed in the United States of America

Mainstay Church Resources' passion is to facilitate
revival among God's people by helping pastors help
people develop healthy spiritual habits in nine vital
areas that always characterize genuine times of spiritual awakening. To support this goal, Mainstay Church
Resources uses a C.H.U.R.C.H. strategy to provide
practical tools and resources, including the annual
50-Day Spiritual Adventure, the Seasonal Advent
Celebration, the 4-Week Festival of Worship, and the
Pastor's Toolbox.

The name "Promise Keepers" and the "PK" crest are
registered trade and service marks of Promise
Keepers, a Colorado nonprofit corporation. The
themes of the Adventure correspond to The Seven
Promises of a Promise Keeper. Copyright © 1994 by
Promise Keepers. Used by permission. All rights
reserved.

CRITTER COUNTY is a registered trademark of
Loveland Communications, Inc. Used by permission.
Critter County was codeveloped by Paula Bussard and
Christine Wyrtzen. Their books and tapes have been
enjoyed by more than a million children across North
America. For additional product or concert informa-
tion, contact: P.O. Box 7, Loveland, OH 45140; (513)
575-4673.

Scriptures marked ICB are taken from the
International Children's Bible, New Century Version,
copyright © 1983, 1986, 1988 by Word Publishing,
Dallas, Texas 75039. Used by permission.

ISBN 1-57849-123-1

*Mainstay Church Resources is not responsible for situations
arising from the use of this curriculum by churches, groups, or
individuals.*

Helping Pastors
Help People Grow

TABLE OF CONTENTS

The Big Picture 5

Ready to Begin:
Administrative Information 9

Ready to Begin:
Weekly Leader Information 13

Tips for Small Group Leaders 21

Sample Project and
Activity Permission Slip 22

Extending the Adventure to a Full 13-Week
Quarter 23

Week 1 Session Plans ...2/14...........................28
  Life Application Page for
  Small Group Leaders 34

Week 2 Session Plans ...2/21..........................36
  Life Application Page for
  Small Group Leaders 41

Week 3 Session Plans ...2/28.........................43
  Life Application Page for
  Small Group Leaders 48

Week 4 Session Plans ...3/7............................50
  Life Application Page for
  Small Group Leaders 55

Week 5 Session Plans ...3/14...........................57
  Life Application Page for
  Small Group Leaders 62

Week 6 Session Plans ...3/21..........................64
  Life Application Page for
  Small Group Leaders 69

Week 7 Session Plans ...3/28...........................71
  Life Application Page for
  Small Group Leaders 76

Week 8 Session Plans ...4/4............................78
  Life Application Page for
  Small Group Leaders 82

Life Application Projects 84

Adventure Song for Kids
  Be Quiet and Know That I Am God 105
  Everyone Wins 109
  Remove the Sin 112
  Honor Your Father and Your Mother..................114
  You Should Meet Together 116
  The Lord Looks at the Heart 118
  Be a Light 120
  Show Me, O God 123

Evaluation Form 127

Order Form 128

NOTES

4

What Is This 50-Day Adventure Curriculum for Children All About?

It's about helping children:

- experience the Bible in a new and exciting way.
- apply stories from Bible times to everyday life today.
- discover what it means to be a Promise Kid.
- learn how to follow God's directions in eight key areas of life.
- learn to love the Lord and his Word.

This Adventure is thematically based, with topics similar to the "Promises Worth Keeping" 50-Day Spiritual Adventure for adults. With permission from the Promise Keepers movement, we have adapted their promises for this Adventure. The overall theme of this Adventure for children is "Promise Kids on the Promise Path: Learning How to Follow God's Directions." The goal of the curriculum is to help each child develop eight traits of a Promise Kid. In this guide the weekly Adventure themes are Promise Path Action Topics that define each lesson. Here is an overview of each Promise Path lesson:

Promise Kids:
1. Stop and think about Jesus

   Bible Story: Luke 10:38–42
   Memory Verse: Psalm 46:10

2. Find friends who help them follow Jesus

   Bible Story: Romans 1:1–12; 16:1–19
   Memory Verse: Proverbs 12:26

3. Do what Jesus would do

   Bible Story: Colossians 3:8–9, 12–13
   Memory Verse: Hebrews 12:1–2

4. Make family time important

   Bible Story: Genesis 50:19–21
   Memory Verse: Ephesians 6:2–3

5. Get involved at church

   Bible Story: Acts 4:32–37; 9:26–28; 13:1–15:35
   Memory Verse: Hebrews 10:25

6. Accept others as Jesus does

   Bible Story: Mark 1:40–42
   Memory Verse: 1 Samuel 16:7

7. Make a difference in their world

   Bible Story: Matthew 5:13–16
   Memory Verse: Matthew 5:16

8. Stay on the Promise Path

   Bible Story: Matthew 28:1–10
   Memory Verse: Psalm 16:11

Each topic will be explored through a creative Bible Story Presentation. To help children experience what it might have been like to hear these truths presented firsthand, children will hear stories from Bible-time characters who will visit through a Bible Time Machine. The Bible Time Machine is found in the Promise Path Factory, the place where everyone works toward discovering traits that help them follow God's directions.

HOW CAN I HELP CHILDREN HAVE A SUCCESSFUL 50-DAY ADVENTURE?

Through the Teaching Methods You Use
Studies show that information learned solely by memorization is forgotten quickly. Therefore, it is our belief that kids learn best when they are actively involved—body, mind, and spirit—in the teaching process. To do this effectively, every child who comes to church or church club should be made to feel welcome. Teachers need to give kids the opportunity to investigate information that interests them, draw conclusions based on the truths of the Bible, and then show what they've learned in a creative manner. This is learning through experience, the teaching approach you'll find used in each of the eight Adventure lessons included in this curriculum. For example:

• Through the use of creative storytelling, Bible Story Time becomes a means for pulling kids into the events being portrayed.

• Through Life Application Projects, kids are given the opportunity to discover for themselves how to apply Bible truths to their everyday life. This approach makes the Bible come alive and have meaning for them. Children are allowed to work alone or with their friends and at their own pace.

• Through the use of Life Application Small Groups, children benefit from hearing one another's perspective on how to apply the Bible story truths they've learned. Talking, praying, and working with the same Small Group each week fosters the growth of friendships and trust.

Through Teamwork and Creativity

Children aren't the only ones to benefit from this instructional style. Teachers are helped, too. They have more time to relate to the children by watching, listening, and asking questions. The lesson format makes it easy to divide and share leadership responsibilities among several adults, as well as utilize individual talents more effectively. For example, some leaders will work on administrative duties while others will supervise a Life Application Project, participate in storytelling, or lead a Small Group (this is an eight-week commitment).

Each activity in this guide should be thought of as a suggestion only. Feel free to add to it or substitute your own creative ideas!

WHO CAN USE THIS CURRICULUM?

This Adventure curriculum material can be used as a weekend children's church or church school program, a midweek program, or a combination thereof. (Information on using this curriculum in different settings starts on p. 18.) The program is designed for kids in grades 1–6, but it can be adapted for kindergartners as well. Most of the curriculum components are written to work with all the elementary grades, whether they meet together or are subdivided in some way. If you're working with a narrower age range, here are some hints to help you find your way through the material:

• The Life Application Projects are organized by age-group, from youngest to oldest.

• In the weekly sessions, note that there is a separate memory verse for younger children (grades K–2).

• On the Life Application Small Group pages, you may find questions for different age levels when appropriate.

This program can work for any size church and any size group—even just one class. (Special tips for

adapting the curriculum to your church size are included on pp. 19–20.) The curriculum also offers recommendations for churches who wish to use it for a full quarter. (Suggestions for utilizing the curriculum during a 13-week quarter can be found on pp. 23–27.)

HOW MAY THIS CURRICULUM BE DIFFERENT FROM OTHERS I'VE USED?

This approach to teaching will require more initial preparation and work than traditional approaches. But most of the work happens before the Adventure begins. For example, you will need to assign Bible Story Time leaders, storytellers, Small Group leaders, and project leaders. You will also need to decide which Life Application Projects to use and gather materials for those projects. You will need to design your Bible Presentation Set and the Promise Path Factory, with help from suggestions that start on page 13.

Whether your congregation is small or large, the curriculum is designed with cooperative teaching in mind. Because often no one person is responsible for the whole session, you're likely to get more volunteers, and the work can be spread around. For example, if there are people in your church who are skilled at drama, they might enjoy working with children on the Life Application Projects that involve dramatic presentation. Teenagers also might welcome a chance to help with projects. The best way to make this program successful is to start getting ready for it well in advance. (See the time line on p. 11.)

WHAT CURRICULUM MATERIALS DO I NEED?

This curriculum and the *Promise Kids Sing-along* cassette are the most important materials you will need. The songs on the sing-along tape are based on all of the Promise Path Memory Verses the kids will learn during this Adventure. This audiocassette may be used as a sing-along help during Song Time. One side of the tape contains the songs with vocals, and one side is accompaniment only.

(Information for ordering the *Promise Kids Sing-along* cassette is on p. 128.)

There is also a music cassette provided for children's home use called *Bug Beepers for Promise Keepers*. This tape contains the same songs as the

Promise Kids Sing-along cassette, but the Bug Beepers tape also includes a Critter County® story line. For ordering information, contact your church's Adventure coordinator, or see page 128 in this guide.

In addition, other resources are available that will help make your Adventure a successful and memorable one. There are two children's books available for home use. Kids in grades 3–6 will use the *Promise Kids on the Promise Path* Children's Journal. Kids in grades K–2 will use the *Bug Beepers for Promise Keepers* Activity Book. Both of these resources reinforce the eight Adventure topics to make learning stick for a lifetime. Kids who use these resources will be more likely to acquire learning that lasts than those who don't use the books.

Both of these books provide the kids with daily activities to help them understand and apply the weekly Adventure topics. If your church hasn't purchased a supply of these books to distribute, make certain the children and their parents know how to get a copy. Check with your church's Adventure coordinator for details, or see page 128 in this leader's guide. Although these two books are designed for home use, each week the children will be asked a question based on their journals during Small Group Time.

HOW IS THE PROGRAM ORGANIZED?

Because the Adventure revolves around the theme of Promise Kids following God's directions, a Promise Path Factory is the vehicle that has been chosen to help students learn about the Bible stories and what it means to be a Promise Kid. The program contains eight weekly sessions that are broken down into three major sections: Life Application Projects, Bible Story Time, and Life Application Small Groups. Each has been designed to help students experience and understand how to follow God's directions and hear speakers such as Jesus' disciples or witnesses of Bible-time events. Additional material has been provided for adaptation to Children's Church Worship, Midweek Programming, and a 13-week quarter. The following information will give you a brief overview of the session segments and their purposes. A more in-depth explanation of how the weekly sessions work is included for Life Application Projects, Bible Story Time, and Life Application Small Groups on pages 13–20.

Three Major Sections

LIFE APPLICATION PROJECTS

Children choose from a variety of projects to work on. Each one teaches kids how to apply and remember the various Bible stories or Promise Path Memory Verses in everyday life.

BIBLE STORY TIME

Children gather together for a presentation that deepens their Bible knowledge and understanding. This section includes:
- Weekly Activities
- Setting the Scene
- Bible Story Presentation
- Comprehension Questions
- Promise Path Memory Verse

LIFE APPLICATION SMALL GROUPS

Children meet in Small Groups to discuss the Bible story and its application to life. Through conversation and prayer they deepen their relationships with each other and with God. This section includes:
- Kid Talk
- Group-Building Activity
- Prayer Talk
- Small Group Tip

Additional Activities for Children's Church Worship or Midweek Programing, and a 13-Week Quarter

CHILDREN'S CHURCH WORSHIP

This weekly section includes:
- Singing
- Critter County Story
- Offering
- Praise and Prayer

MIDWEEK EXTRAS

This weekly section includes:
- A featured game (see "Game" section each week)
- Singing
- Critter County Story

13-WEEK QUARTER

This section includes suggestions for lengthening the curriculum to fill a 13-week quarter. You can plan five weeks before or after the eight-week Adventure. Or, you may arrange the additional sessions any way you wish to meet your needs. This information is found on pages 23–27, and includes:

- Five Additional Bible Stories to Reinforce Promise Path Topics
- Five Additional Promise Path Memory Verses
- Six Additional Life Application Projects

HOW LONG DO I SPEND ON EACH PART OF THE SESSION?

The amount of time you allot to each segment of a session is up to you. Each week's session can be used as a one-hour or two-hour program or something in-between. The following chart shows how churches might allot time to four different program settings. These are just suggestions and may be altered as needed.

Session Segments	Sunday School	Children's Church	Midweek Program	Combined Sunday School/Children's Church
Life Application Projects	20 min.	15 min.	40 min.	40 min.
Bible Story Time	20 min.	15 min.	25 min.	25 min.
Life Application Small Groups	20 min.	15 min.	25 min.	25 min.
Children's Church Worship	——	15 min.	——	25 min.
Midweek Extras	——	——	30 min.	10 min. (Game)

Children may move through the three main parts of a lesson in any way you choose. For example, the routine could be something like this:

1. Check-in

2. Life Application Projects

3. Bible Story Time

OR

4. Life Application Small Groups

5. Dismissal

1. Check-in

2. Bible Story Time

3. Life Application Small Groups

4. Life Application Projects

5. Dismissal

WHAT PREPLANNING NEEDS TO BE DONE?

Plan to have one leader for each of the three main sections of the session: Bible Story Time, Life Application Projects, and Life Application Small Groups. For a small church or single class, the same person may coordinate all three parts. For a larger church, you'll also need an administrative leader. Utilize the Planning Time Line on page 11 to make this Adventure happen. Because the majority of the work is done before the Adventure begins, this time line is crucial for ensuring the success of your program. To tailor the curriculum to best fit your congregation, see the section titled "How Can the Materials Be Adapted for Use in Small and Large Churches?" on pages 19–20.

WHAT ARE THE DUTIES OF THE STAFF?

Life Application Project leader(s) will:
- Determine how many projects to offer. One project should be made available for every 10–12 kids. If your group is small, always offer at least two projects so children have a choice.
- Decide which projects to offer and for how many weeks.
- Gather materials needed to accomplish each project.
- Provide a question or two to help kids tie the project to everyday life.
- Supervise each activity—one adult or older teen at every project site is ideal.
- Oversee project cleanup.
- Store projects and materials between sessions.

Bible Story Time leader(s) will:
- Welcome children to the Promise Path Factory and Bible Story Time.
- Create the presentation atmosphere of the Promise Path Factory, Bible Time Machine, and Conveyor Belt.
- Set the weekly scene.
- Lead into and/or participate in the storytelling presentation.
- Ask comprehension questions as a follow-up.
- Present the Promise Path Memory Verses and related activities.

Small Group leader(s) will:
- Sit with their group of six to eight children during the story presentation.
- Meet with their group during each session.
- Build a supportive relationship with the kids.
- Help children apply Bible truths to their own lives by working through the Life Application pages in this guide.
- Touch base with children in their group during project time.

Administrative leader(s) will:
- Keep attendance.
- Provide name tags.
- Provide maps, routing, and signs.
- Provide photocopied materials for leaders of other sections.

HOW WILL I DIVIDE THE CHILDREN INTO GROUPS?

Before the Adventure begins, divide the kids into Small Groups of six to eight members. This same group of six to eight will stay together throughout the Adventure, splitting up only to work on Life Application Projects. They will meet weekly with their Small Group leader during each session. You may divide them by grade, by gender, or divide them randomly. Keep in mind that the children in grades K–2 have a different journal at home than the kids in grades 3–6. Though they don't bring their journals to church, the kids will have an opportunity to talk about them during the Small Group Time discussions.

WHERE WILL I PUT THE KIDS FOR THE DIFFERENT PARTS OF THE SESSIONS?

Life Application Projects
Life Application Project work sites are set up to accommodate 10–12 kids each. Each site should be stocked with suitable materials and supplies and the needed work space to complete each project. They can be set up as various stations in a large room setting, or they can take place in a number of small rooms where traffic can flow through easily. If your church congregation is small, see suggestions for adaptation on pages 19–20 of this book.

It would be wise to use permission slips for some of the Life Application Projects. Refer to the sample on page 22 for ideas you can adapt to your situation.

Bible Story Time

If possible, bring all the kids together in one large group for the Bible Story Presentation. Try to create a casual, nonschool atmosphere for the Adventure sessions. Have the kids sit on the floor in a carpeted room, on carpet squares, or on area rugs that can be rolled up. If you are limited in space and the Life Application Projects have been set up in your large group area, move the project worktables to the sides or to the back of the room to create space. You may also want to decorate the area to look like a Promise Path Factory to give the children a visual element that will help your lessons come alive. Suggestions for creating the Promise Path Factory setting are found on pages 13–15 in Bible Story Time setup.

Life Application Small Groups

Select interesting and unusual places for the Small Groups to meet. Small places in and around the building that have a hideout or clubhouse feel to them work best. You could even consider putting up freestanding tents in the classroom. Other places might include the corner of a hallway, a stage, empty space under a large stairwell, or even separate corners of your large group area. Make sure that kids know where the nearest exits are in case of an emergency. Pick areas that are somewhat close to the large group area. The kids should be able to get to their Small Group locations quickly. Encourage the kids to sit on the floor in a circle so they can talk to each other freely.

HOW DO I ORGANIZE THE WEEKLY SESSIONS?

Attendance

Position your attendance table(s) in a convenient place near the main entrance. Keep in mind that kids will need to be able to line up without causing a traffic jam. Hang a sign or banner that says "Promise Kids on the Promise Path Start Here!" or "The 50-Day Adventure Starts Here!" on the front of the table or the wall behind it. If you have a large number of kids to check in, you may want to set up more than one table to speed up the process. You can color code the check-in sites to correspond with the kids' colored name tags, as described in the "Name Tags" section below.

Use whatever method of record-keeping best fits your situation. If your group is small in number, you can use one large attendance chart for everyone. If your group is large, you might prefer to use a separate attendance chart or book for each Small Group. This will work particularly well if you choose to group the children by their normal class or grade divisions.

The children should check in each week upon arrival to record their attendance and pick up their name tags. Ask an adult or dependable teen to work at the same attendance table each week.

Name Tags

Color-coded name tags can help the kids quickly locate their Small Groups and learn others' names. In addition to a child's name and his or her group's color, a name tag can include the group leader's name and the location of each Small Group. This is especially helpful in large churches where newcomers may need extra help finding where they belong. Be sure to provide name tags for all the adults taking part in the program. The Small Group leaders could wear color-coded name tags to match those of their assigned kids.

You can purchase adhesive-backed or plastic folder name tags at an office supply store. Color code them by using construction paper in different colors or colored markers. Ask the group leaders to gather the name tags at the end of each week's session for reuse the next week.

Small Group Names

Although you could simply refer to the groups by their color names, you might want to add to the Adventure by letting each group select its own name. If possible, have the names relate to this year's Adventure by creating factory or promise-related identities. Or you can choose names such as the 12 tribes of Israel or the names of the disciples.

Transitions and Traffic Flow

In order to prevent chaos, you need to think things through ahead of time when planning to move groups of children from one place to another. For example, at the end of the Bible Story Time, when you are about to dismiss the kids to their Small Groups, it's a lot less chaotic if you dismiss the groups one at a time with thought to their destinations. Let the groups who have the longest walk leave first. Make the "Rules of the Road" perfectly clear during the first session. If kids need to be quiet as they pass certain locations, let them know that before they get there. If they need to stay with their leader and not rush ahead, make that clear too. Kids will usually give you the behavior you expect if you make your expectations clear.

PLANNING TIME LINE

Twelve Weeks Before the Adventure
1. Purchase children's curriculum materials.

2. Determine in what setting you will use the materials (children's church, Sunday school, or midweek club).

3. Establish a planning committee and an overall administrator for the Adventure.

4. Confirm the children's Adventure dates to coordinate with the adult program and your regular children's program schedule.

5. Pray for God's help and guidance.

Eight Weeks Before the Adventure
1. Estimate the number of students who will participate in the Adventure.

2. Recruit storytellers, Bible Story Time leaders, Small Group leaders (one for every 6–8 children), Life Application Project leaders (one for every 10–12 children), and administrative leaders.

3. Make arrangements and recruit staff for Children's Church Worship or midweek programs, if needed.

4. Recruit leaders to supervise registration and publicity for the Adventure.

5. Set a date for a planning meeting.

Six Weeks Before the Adventure
1. Hold a planning meeting with the people who will be involved in making this Adventure happen. Include all of the recruited leaders.

2. Distribute a calendar of events. Include future planning and training meetings, Adventure start-up and finish dates, and the Adventure cleanup and evaluation dates.

3. Determine how many Life Application Projects to offer, which ones, and for how many weeks. (See the section for Life Application Project leaders under "What Are the Duties of the Staff?" on p. 9.)

4. Determine how supplies for Life Application Projects will be purchased and/or collected, and who will be responsible for them.

5. Assign work sites to project leaders.

6. Decide how and where you will set up your story-telling area. Suggestions for setting up a Promise Path Factory are found on pages 13–15. Make a list of the materials you will need and assign leaders who will be responsible for setup.

7. Determine how attendance will be kept and the locations for Bible Story Time, Life Application Projects, and Small Group meetings.

8. Decide how children will be divided.

Four Weeks Before the Adventure
1. Invite students to the Adventure. Publicize it in your church bulletin and newsletter.

2. Check with storytellers, Bible Story Time leaders, Life Application Project leaders, and administrative leaders to make certain of the following:
   • Project materials are being obtained.
   • Maps to session locations are being made.
   • Photocopies of materials have been distributed.
   • Name tags are being made.
   • Stories are being rehearsed.
   • The Promise Path Factory is being prepared.
   • Storytellers are obtaining costumes for their performances.

3. Begin your publicity campaign and reach out to your community with an invitation to the Adventure. Work with your churchwide Adventure coordinator and publicity chairperson.

4. Begin early registration.

5. Assign Small Group locations. Encourage Small Group leaders to decorate their space or room as desired if it won't interfere with someone else sharing their space.

Two Weeks Before the Adventure
1. Organize project materials. Label work areas and storage spaces (if needed).

2. Review maps, making any necessary changes. Design signs to route participants to appropriate areas.

3. Organize name tags for check-in.

4. Begin setting up the Promise Path Factory, if possible.

5. Create a checklist for each part of your session.

6. Check in with your leaders to review their last-minute needs or concerns.

7. Establish Small Groups of children.

One Week Before the Adventure

1. Set up project areas, making sure:
   • You have all the necessary materials.
   • Directions are posted for children to follow.
   • Storage areas are ready for safekeeping of projects.
   • Questions are posted connecting projects to everyday life.

2. Complete the Promise Path Factory. Be sure you have created a Bible Time Machine and a Conveyor Belt to produce the Promise Path Memory Verse.

3. Touch base with storytellers. Make certain they have all costumes, props, and materials needed for their presentations.

4. Check in with Small Group leaders. Make sure they have the Life Application pages for the Small Group meetings. Answer any last-minute questions.

5. Set up your registration table. Have available maps and name tags for check-in.

READY TO BEGIN: WEEKLY LEADER INFORMATION

This section will be a walk-through of one weekly session in detail. Refer to the actual Week 1 session, starting on page 28, for more help in understanding the weekly sessions.

WHAT IS THE OVERVIEW?

For your convenience, an overview box is printed at the top of the first page of each session. It is intended to give you a quick picture of the session's Promise Path Action Topic, Bible story basis, the Promise Path Memory Verse, and the Desired Outcome for each lesson. This will allow you to quickly check what's coming up in the session as well as review what has already been presented. Here's a sample from Week 1:

SAMPLE WEEK

WEEK ONE OVERVIEW

- **Promise Path Action Topic:** Promise Kids Stop and Think About Jesus
- **Desired Outcome:** That the children will learn to take a small amount of time each day to stop and think about Jesus, through prayer, Bible reading, music, quiet time, or other appropriate activities.
- **Bible Story:** Luke 10:38–42
- **Promise Path Memory Verse:** God says, "Be quiet and know that I am God. I will be supreme over all the nations. I will be supreme in the earth." Psalm 46:10 (ICB) (older children); God says, "Be quiet and know that I am God." Psalm 46:10 (ICB) (younger children)
- **Bible Story Presentation:** Story told by Martha
- **Life Application Projects:** The Life Application Projects that relate specifically to the Promise Path Action Topic for Week 1 are Promise Path Prayer Book (p. 92) and Promise Path Sculpture (p. 102).

WHAT DO THE TEACHING/ LEARNING COMPONENTS LOOK LIKE IN DETAIL?

Life Application Projects

The Life Application Projects may be done at the beginning of each weekly session or at the end. But there are a few distinct advantages to doing them first. The projects can be set up and ready to go at least 20 minutes before the official start of your session. That way the kids who arrive early, such as the children of the program staff members, will have a learning activity to do right away.

You'll need to pay careful attention to the time allotted for each project. Let the kids know the first session that in most cases they will have many weeks to finish their projects. Explain cleanup responsibilities, and be sure to cue them when it is time to put things away and gather for Bible Story Time or when it is time to conclude the session. More information on Life Application Projects is included in this curriculum on pages 84–104.

Because some of the projects involve activities such as nailing or using needles, it would be wise to have parents sign a permission slip before the Adventure begins. See page 22 for a sample slip.

Bible Story Time

SETUP

The Bible story or lesson during the 50-Day Adventure can be presented at the start or during the middle of your session. If you offer the story first, you may wish to include some of the songs found on the *Promise Kids Sing-along* cassette. That way you can offer music as a welcome, and stragglers won't miss the story.

The Bible Story Presentation is designed to be done by costumed storytellers. If the space is available, and you so choose, bring all of the kids together in one large group for the Bible Story Presentation. The members of each Small Group should sit with their leader. This will scatter the adults throughout the whole group, making discipline easier. If there are a lot of children in your program, it's helpful to have the Small Group leaders gather up their kids and bring them to the story area.

The Promise Path stories are all presented in a Promise Path Factory, where everyone works on making things that help them learn how to follow God's directions. You may choose to create a Promise Path Factory to help your presentations come alive for children and add to the fun. The Promise Path Factory has two important elements: the Bible Time Machine and the Conveyor Belt. The Bible Time Machine is the vehicle that enables Bible-time characters to come and tell the Bible story. The Conveyor Belt is the instrument used in producing each week's Promise Path Memory Verse. Some of the Life Application Projects offer activities that can be used for the storytelling time.

Here are several suggestions and illustrations for setting up your Promise Path Factory:

FACTORY DESIGN

There are a variety of ways to set up your Promise Path Factory. There is no need to limit yourself to the suggestions provided if you have a creative team that wants to enrich the Promise Path Factory with its own ideas!

Because the Promise Path Factory focuses on following God's directions, a weekly directional sign has been established to complement the Promise Path Action Topics. These directionals include:
- Week 1: Stop sign (Stop and think about Jesus).
- Week 2: Pedestrian Crossing sign (Find friends who help you follow Jesus).
- Week 3: Stoplight (Stop, Caution, and Go to do what Jesus would do).
- Week 4: Construction Zone Ahead (Family Builders working to make family time important).
- Week 5: Merge sign (Get involved at church).
- Week 6: Slippery Road Ahead sign (Accept others as Jesus does).
- Week 7: Walk sign (Make a difference in your world).
- Week 8: Yield sign (Take the time to slow down so you can stay on the Promise Path).

These directionals can be designed as typical street signs that hang in various locations around the Promise Path Factory to generate interest in upcoming topics. These signs will also be used to introduce the Bible story each week.

To further enhance your Promise Path Factory atmosphere, create buttons, levers, and wheels to hang in various locations around the room. You will also need to build a Bible Time Machine and a

Conveyor Belt. Instructions for those are found below.

BIBLE TIME MACHINE

You will need one or two large refrigerator boxes big enough to house two people. Begin by connecting the boxes to create one unit. Be sure the box has the rear cut out or a door for storytellers to get in and out. Then paint the box a bright color and label it "Bible Time Machine." Decorate it by painting and/or attaching various knobs on it. Cut a 9" slit toward the top from which a strip of long paper can be pulled. This will be the mail slot. Prepare a clear sign of the weekly Promise Path Action Topic to be pulled from this slot during each session. Hang a set of

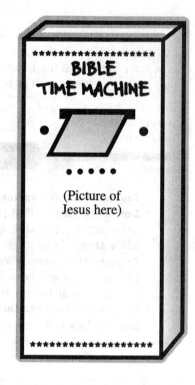

flashing Christmas lights to outline the machine. Arrange to have it plugged into the wall where it cannot be seen. When you press a button to activate the machine, give a verbal cue that will notify the person inside the box or off stage to plug in the lights. Turn the lights off when the machine is shut down.

CONVEYOR BELT

To make a Conveyor Belt, you will need a long rectangular table, a 3/4" diameter wooden dowel, knobs for wheels, a paper roll, and

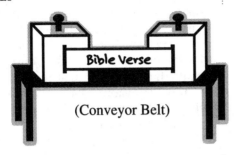

(Conveyor Belt)

two boxes, each approximately 25" square. The boxes will be located at each end of the table and should be large enough to house a roll of paper but small enough to fit on the table without falling off. (If you have a willing carpenter, you may wish to build this out of wood. It will be sturdier and will last longer.) Follow these steps to complete the Conveyor Belt:

1. Paint each box a bright color. Cut a slit 1" larger than the width of your paper roll at each end of the box. (See diagram.)
2. Purchase a roll of paper no wider than 20", or create one by taping 8 1/2" x 14" paper together to create a long strip. Write each week's Promise Path Memory Verse on the roll, in order, leaving about 3' of blank space between each verse. Print in bold letters so that it can be read from the audience. Do not use a longer space than you have to work with between your boxes for each verse. Leave approximately 3 yards of blank space at the beginning and end of your roll. (The back of the box can be removed to make it easier to work with the paper.)
3. Measure two small circles 3/4" in diameter in the center of the top and bottom of each box. Cut out one circle at the top end of each box.
4. Slip a 3/4" dowel rod through the hole in each box. It should stick out approximately 6 inches. You will have to cut it to size accordingly.
5. Attach the end of your paper roll to the dowel rod in the right-hand box and tape securely in place. Be sure your writing is right side up. Roll the paper up tightly around the rod. Then feed it through the slit in the box.
6. Gently pull the paper roll over to the other box, feed it through the slit, and then secure it to the dowel rod in that box by taping it securely in

place. Because you left the first 3 yards of your roll blank, there will be no writing showing.
7. Attach a knob to the end of each dowel rod to make cranking the belt easier.
8. Decorate as desired.
9. To operate, crank each end of the dowel rods to roll the Promise Path Memory Verse into view.

FIVE MAIN ACTIVITIES

A. Weekly Activities

Open with a few welcoming comments and announcements, birthday recognitions, and the collection of an offering. (If you are using this curriculum with children's church, you may prefer to wait until your worship time to collect an offering.) Try to keep these opening activities brief.

B. Setting the Scene

During the first week's session, you may use the "Setting the Scene" time to explain what the Adventure is about. Then in the following weeks, this time can be used to review the previous week's Promise Path Action Topic or to prepare the kids for the Bible Story Presentation. Once again, try to keep this section short. (Please note that the general instructions for this section are printed in regular type and the suggestions for things you might say to the kids are printed in **bold** type.)

C. Bible Story Presentation

Most of the Adventure Bible stories are written as a storytelling drama for one or two adults or teens. All of the stories are based on the Adventure Promise Path Action Topics. If you choose to present the story to the combined group rather than to individual grade-level classes, you will need to recruit fewer people to act as storytellers. (For Week 8, there is a suggested alternative student drama that can be completed as a Life Application Project.) Four or five adults or teens can take turns handling the storytelling responsibility. That way the same people won't have to present the Bible story every week. Of course, if you have other ideas on how to present the Bible story, please feel free to put them into action! The material in this curriculum is meant to spark your creativity, not to limit it.

Each of the Bible characters that tell the stories is introduced through the Bible Time Machine. The leader will first retrieve the Promise Path Action Topic from the mail slot. Then, after some discussion with the group, the Bible Time Machine is put into action and will produce the Bible-time storyteller for that day.

Encourage your storytellers to try to act and talk like the Bible characters they are portraying. Encourage them to learn their lines well enough to perform them without a script in hand. If you have difficulty recruiting people who are willing or able to do this, you can revise the scripts so that they are read by a narrator while other individuals mime the action. You can also revise the stories slightly so that the characters can hold their scripts on clipboards or scrolls.

The use of costumes is recommended. A simple way to imitate Bible-time clothing is to take a length of fabric (plain or striped) about 8' x 4', cut a hole for the head in the center, and tie the waist with a scarf, necktie, or rope. A pair of sandals and a head-band or scarf will add the finishing touches.

While you want to encourage the characters to be natural and ad-lib a bit, they need to be mindful of time. The skits are intended to be presented in three to five minutes. To help your storytellers keep within the time limit, make certain there is a clock in their view, or arrange for someone to give them a signal when it's time to wrap things up.

D. Comprehension Questions

In order to help you get a feel for what the children have learned from the story presentation, this curriculum includes comprehension questions to use as a follow-up to each session's story. These are just a few direct questions to make sure the kids understand the main points of the Bible story. Be certain

to allow the kids time to think before answering each question, but keep in mind that a large group is not the best setting for holding a full-scale discussion with kids. Save the application discussion for Life Application Small Groups.

E. Promise Path Memory Verse

This is the time kids will be introduced to the eight Adventure memory verses. Each verse is related to the weekly Promise Path Action Topic. As added fun during each Bible Story Time, volunteers will be given the chance to crank the Conveyor Belt levers with the Bible verse for that session.

The session plans include a suggestion on how to present each of the weekly verses to a large group in a way that is both fun and effective. These activities will help the kids to better understand the meaning of the verse as well as how to apply it and memorize it. You will also find suggestions for adapting these activities to teach the younger children (grades K–2) a shortened version of the verse. If you have room in your Bible story area, you can have the older children and younger children move to opposite sides of the room so they can work on their verses without bothering each other. If not, consider dismissing the children in grades K–2 earlier than the older

 kids so that the younger children can work on their verses at their Small Group sites. Look for this icon to help you easily locate the verse variation for younger children.

Life Application Small Groups

THE OVERVIEW

For your convenience, an overview box is printed at the top of the Life Application page in each session. It is intended to give you a quick picture of the Promise Path Action Topic, Bible story, Desired Outcome, Promise Path Memory Verse, and a list of things you'll need during your Small Group time.

Here's a sample from Week 1.

LIFE APPLICATION PAGE

For Small Group Leaders
• WEEK ONE •

- **Promise Path Action Topic:** Stop and Think About Jesus
- **Desired Outcome:** That the children will learn to take a small amount of time each day to stop and think about Jesus through prayer, Bible reading, music, quiet time, or other appropriate activities.
- **Bible Story:** Luke 10:38–42
- **Promise Path Memory Verse:** God says, "Be quiet and know that I am God. I will be supreme over all the nations. I will be supreme in the earth." Psalm 46:10 (ICB) (older children); God says, "Be quiet and know that I am God." Psalm 46:10 (ICB) (younger children)

THINGS YOU'LL NEED

- Copy of "Tips for Small Group Leaders" (p. 21)
- *Bug Beepers for Promise Keepers* Critter County Activity Book (K–2)
- *Promise Kids on the Promise Path* Children's Journal (3–6)
- Promise Kids Prayer Poster
- Promise Path Action Topic Poster
- Newsprint
- Markers
- Chalkboard and chalk

IN ADVANCE

Make a poster using the Promise Kids Prayer found on page 21. Also make a Promise Path Action Topic poster showing a picture of your church with the topics printed on paths leading from the church (see illustration below).

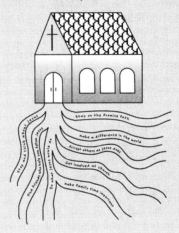

SETUP

The Life Application Small Group section, which comes after the Bible Story Presentation, may be done during the middle portion or at the end of each session.

During this time the children are encouraged to draw a connection between the message of the Bible story and its application to their lives. A Small Group led by a friendly, caring adult makes it easier for shy or quiet children to risk sharing their private thoughts and feelings. This activity is best done in Small Groups (in their own special place) where the kids can feel comfortable enough to reflect on and discuss what they have learned.

MATERIALS

A reproducible Life Application page for Small Group leaders is included in this curriculum at the end of the instructions for each weekly session. (See the first weekly page on p. 34.)

The Life Application pages are intended to provide Small Group leaders with the information they need to conduct successful group times. The pages include questions to ask the kids, explanations of each Promise Path Action Topic, prayer reminders, challenges that fit the session objectives, a group-building activity, and tips to make the Small Group time more effective.

You will need to make copies of these pages to give to the Small Group leaders. You will need to distribute each Life Application page at least one week ahead of time or as a collection in a folder, so that the Small Group leaders will be able to prepare for the sessions at home.

Each group leader will also need to make a Promise Kids Prayer Poster and a Promise Path Action Topic Poster with a picture of your church. The picture of your church can be an actual photograph that is enlarged, or a creative representation of it. From the church, create eight different paths leading out of it, with each path containing a Promise Path Action Topic.

WHAT ELSE IS AVAILABLE FOR CHILDREN'S CHURCH WORSHIP OR A MIDWEEK PROGRAM?

Children's Church Worship
The extra components included for this option are:

SINGING

Songs based on the Promise Path Memory Verses are included in this curriculum beginning on page 105. The same songs are included on the *Promise Kids Sing-along* cassette that you may use in place of live accompaniment. Piano and guitar accompaniment are included in this book. To order the sing-along cassette, see page 128.

If times allows, you may also want to include a few familiar songs that relate to the weekly Promise Path Action Topics. If your children's music collection needs a bit of updating, check out what's new at your local Christian bookstore. Two popular children's songwriters are Mary Rice Hopkins and Rob Evans.

CRITTER COUNTY STORY

The children who have been on a 50-Day Adventure in years past will be familiar with the Critter County characters. Other children may also know them through the popular children's music tapes based on the Critter County series. Although these stories (based on the weekly topics) are written for younger children, their brevity and humor may mean that older children enjoy them, too. These familiar Critter County characters will encourage the children to become Promise Kids by following God's directions.

OFFERING

Scripture calls the practice of bringing to God monetary offerings an act of worship. You may want to give the kids a chance to worship God in this manner. If you do, consider something more than just asking the kids to place their money in a collection plate or basket. Encourage them to thank God out loud for one of his blessings each time they place an offering in the basket, or suggest that they bring a food item for your local food pantry. (Children who don't have a monetary offering to give can still take part by thanking God for something when the offering basket passes them.)

PRAISE AND PRAYER

The praise and prayer suggestions are intended to give children the opportunity to praise God as a group. You will find a variety of prayer ideas suggested to help kids learn how to pray and to help them feel comfortable praying aloud.

Midweek Extras
The extra components for this option are as follows:

GAME

Games are an important tool in teaching children to cooperate and follow directions in an entertaining way. Also, a well-constructed game can help reinforce the point of a lesson. But we know, as you do, that few games are equally good for all ages, all settings, and all time frames. That's why we offer suggestions on how to adapt the games to different situations. Many of the games are of a cooperative, rather than competitive, nature. These games encourage physical activity and fun without creating winners and losers. Of course, you can choose to substitute game ideas of your own if you desire.

Although safety is an assumption, you would be wise to have parents sign a permission slip before children play any of the games. See page 22 for a sample slip.

CRITTER COUNTY STORY

After an active game, let your kids cool off in Critter County, where something interesting is always taking place. Children who have been on a 50-Day Adventure before will be familiar with the Critter County characters, and they'll enjoy helping their friends get to know them, too. Each week's tale is based on the weekly Promise Path Action Topic. These brief stories are written for early elementary children, but older children may benefit from them, too. The charming critters have a way of capturing everybody's interest while helping children discover how to follow God's directions.

SINGING

You can reinforce the Promise Path Memory Verses and Promise Path Action Topics by teaching the songs included in this book, beginning on page 105. The *Promise Kids Sing-along* cassette is a good option for situations where there is no live accompaniment. To order copies of the tape, see page 128. You will probably also want to use a few songs the children already know. Help them learn to view group singing as a pleasant time of celebration and worship.

HOW CAN THE MATERIALS BE ADAPTED FOR USE IN SMALL AND LARGE CHURCHES?

The material in this curriculum may be used by an individual teacher in a small class or by a team of several teachers with lots of kids. Whether your church is of the small, medium, or large variety, the 50-Day Adventure can work for you. The following tips will help you adapt the material to your setting.

Small Churches

Small churches usually face the twin challenges of limited staff and limited space when planning special programs for kids. These challenges can be overcome with ingenuity. Here are some suggestions:

• The Life Application Projects that require more time or special facilities are tagged with this symbol: You may want to adapt or avoid those projects. However, at least half of the projects take little setup, cleanup, and storage. Focus on them if you have space limitations. Another way to deal with a smaller space is to offer only two or three Life Application Project options at a time. Then, when the kids complete them, you can introduce two or three new ones.

• To make storage easier, try to obtain a large cart on wheels. Store individual projects in inexpensive storage units that are clearly labeled. Use another cart shelf to pile projects that need to be laid flat. Then wheel the cart off to a storage space after project time, and it will be easy to return project materials for use again the following week.

• The ideal staffing for the Adventure is to have different people work in each section of the program. However, it may be easier for you to incorporate the program into a classroom setting. If that is the case, the teacher can present the Bible story, select two of the Life Application Projects to do, and then use the Life Application Small Group activities with the class at the end of each session.

You may wish to ask leaders to play duplicate leadership roles. A project leader can serve as a Life Application Small Group leader. Or you may have a Small Group leader who would also like to tell one of the stories. Choose whatever combination works best for your staff and setting.

• Combining the children into one group for Bible Story Time will reduce the number of people needed to present the weekly dramas. Senior citizens and teens might love the opportunity to put their acting skills to use.

• If you have 30 or fewer children, divide your kids into two separate age groups. Provide two different rooms for each part of the Adventure. Half of the group can meet in the Bible story room, while the other half meets in the Life Application Project room. (Offer two or three projects each week.) One-third of the way through your session, ask the groups to switch rooms. The leaders can remain the same in each room. Complete the session by using the rooms the children are already in for Life Application Small Groups.

Large Churches

Large churches not only have a bigger talent pool to draw from for staffing, they also have more children to work with. The challenge for large churches can be one of commitment, space, and organization. In the large church, the sense of being needed is diminished by the assumption that there is someone else around to do the job. People look for short-term, convenient assignments because they know there are lots of other people available to lend a hand. Here are some suggestions for making your Adventure a positive and well-organized learning experience:

• This 50-Day Adventure for kids allows you to subdivide the duties in many ways. Individuals can commit to working on one activity or project each week or to working just a couple of weeks. Different people will be attracted to storytelling, creative projects, music, games, and record-keeping activities.

• There are two positions that need to filled by people willing to make an eight-week commitment: the Adventure administrator and the Small Group leaders. Look for people who want a sense of being needed for these roles. One of the goals of the Life Application Small Group is to develop a relationship between the kids and a caring Christian role model, someone with whom they'll become comfortable enough to share their thoughts and feelings and to partner with in prayer. This won't happen if a new face shows up each week in the role of a Small Group leader. Ask God to help you find the people he has equipped for this task. If you show them how much they are needed, an eight-week commitment should be no problem.

• To avoid first-day confusion, hold a registration day for your Adventure in advance. This way you can preassign most children to Small Groups before your

Adventure begins as well as be prepared for the numbers you will receive.

• Provide several registration check-in tables for children to go to as they enter each week. Label them with letters of the alphabet, by Small Group names, or by grade.

• Clearly mark out the areas children are expected to sit in during Bible Story Time. This can be done by placing tape on the floor, labeling rows with signs, or hanging Small Group names above their assigned areas.

• If you have a number of people who wish to participate in the storytelling time, expand the dramas to include other characters, such as crowd members or news reporters. Encourage others to get involved with set decoration, prop collection, and costuming. Provide your storytellers with a costume rack that is easily accessible and well stocked with various-sized tunics, scarves, belts, sandals, wigs, and beards.

• If you will be offering a variety of Life Application Projects that must be stored in one room, provide each leader with a large bin for his or her supplies. Label each bin with the leader's name and the Life Application Project title.

• To avoid confusion, post clearly marked maps and schedules around your meeting area that children and parents can easily follow to get where they need to go. Label each Small Group space with the leader's name and the Small Group name, if there is one.

Life Application Small Groups provide the children and you a chance to retreat to a quiet place to talk and pray together. Small Groups should have between six and eight children in them. The children you are assigned on the first day will remain in your group during the whole Adventure. This means that it is important for you to commit to taking part in each week's session. The two main goals of your Small Group Time are as follows:

• To help the children apply truths from the Bible story that will guide them in: a) making decisions about their relationship with Jesus, and b) discovering how to follow God's directions.
• To help the children develop faith-building relationships with a Christian adult (you) and with a group of Christian peers (the other kids in your Small Group).

You will be given a "Life Application Page for Small Group Leaders" for each of the eight weekly Adventure sessions. These pages include information to help you accomplish the Small Group goals. Each page has four sections:

KID TALK

This section provides questions for leaders to ask to begin a guided discussion. These are open-ended questions that encourage children to think and talk about how to apply the Bible lesson to their lives. This is not a time to retell the Bible story or to tell the kids what the point of the lesson is. Think of your role as leading the children to the discovery of insights, rather than dispensing knowledge.

The Kid Talk section is also a time to discuss the weekly Promise Path Action Topic and Desired Outcome. To help your kids review the topics, you might list each topic on a separate path that stretches out from a picture of your church and into the world at large (see details on p. 17).

GROUP-BUILDING ACTIVITY

This section provides you with an activity that will promote a community spirit within your Small Group. These activities are short games or trust-building exercises that will provide the kids with a comfortable and enjoyable avenue for sharing with one another.

PRAYER TALK

This section gives you and the children the opportunity to develop an interest in praying as a group and praying for each other. Begin by making a Promise Kids Prayer Poster that fits your age-group. (See the prayer below.) Then use the Promise Kids Prayer each week. Also remember to ask the kids if they have any prayer requests. (It often helps them open up if you share a concern of your own and ask them to pray for you.) As you get to know each other better, you can encourage them to take turns praying short sentence prayers.

PROMISE KIDS PRAYER

Dear Jesus,
I want to live like a Promise Kid by
following your directions.
But sometimes I don't know what to do.
Teach me how to follow you.
Help me _____
(name something for which
you need God's help).
In your name,
Amen.

SMALL GROUP TIP

This section provides Small Group Tips to help you understand your group's needs so that you can create a comfortable setting for spiritual growth.

(Form to be adapted or photocopied)

Dear Parent,

For *(number)* weeks beginning on *(date)*, your child will be participating in an exciting 50-Day Adventure at Sunday school *(or children's church, church club, etc.)*. This program will include Life Application Projects, creative Bible Story Presentations, Life Application Small Groups, and games.

Your child will have the chance to choose from a variety of Life Application Projects and Bible-related games. Some of the projects involve sewing, carpentry, using hammers and nails, baking, and using scissors. Some of the supervised games involve running and throwing activities. *(Customize both of these to fit the projects and games you've chosen.)* Supervision will be provided at all times by adults or older teens.

Please sign this permission slip and return it to *(name)* by *(date)*. If there are activities you would prefer your child did not participate in, please note them below.

Name of child: _____

Please excuse from the following activities: _____

_____

Name of child: _____

Please excuse from the following activities: _____

_____

Name of child: _____

Please excuse from the following activities: _____

_____

Name of parent/guardian: _____

Signature: _____   Date: _____

WHAT IF I WANT TO EXTEND THE ADVENTURE TO A FULL 13-WEEK QUARTER?

EXTENDING THE ADVENTURE

The extra components for this option have been developed to offer churches the opportunity to use this curriculum to fill a 13-week quarter. Below are suggestions for five additional sessions. Each centers around and further develops one of the eight Promise Path Action Topics. Use the options as you see fit, sequencing as many sessions as you wish before or after the eight core Adventure sessions. Each optional session will provide you with:

- A Promise Path Action Topic
- A Scripture text that can be incorporated into a Bible Story Presentation
- A suggested storyteller
- A Promise Path Memory Verse

There are six additional Life Application Projects to explore as well.

The suggestions included here are jumping-off points to help you create your own sessions for the extra five weeks. You can continue to use the Promise Path Factory and Bible Time Machine as the backdrop for the lesson introduction and Bible Story Presentation. For Life Application Projects, use the ideas below, or offer projects from this curriculum that you don't plan to use during the eight-week Adventure.

Two good resources for detailed project instructions and supply lists are *Incredibly Awesome Crafts for Kids* (Des Moines, Iowa: Better Homes and Gardens Books, 1992) and *Crafts for Kids: A Month-by-Month Idea Book*, by Barbara L. Dondiego (second ed., Blue Ridge Summit, Penn.: Tab Books, 1991). These books are excellent resources for papercraft and puppet-making projects. You can find both at your local library. Bookstores like Borders, Crown Books, or your local Christian bookstore will have good resources for crafts and activities as well.

Be sure to have an extra adult or older teen supervising when children use sharp scissors, needles, or tools of any kind. You will be wise to have parents sign a permission slip (sample on p. 22) for any projects offered.

OPTIONAL SESSION 1

Promise Path Action Topic: Promise Kids Find Friends Who Help Them Follow Jesus

Bible Story: 1 Samuel 20:1–17, David & Jonathan

Storyteller: David or Jonathan telling about the importance of their friendship and following God

Promise Path Memory Verse: Whoever spends time with wise people will become wise. Proverbs 13:20 (ICB) (all children)

OPTIONAL SESSION 2

Promise Path Action Topic: Promise Kids Do What Jesus Would Do

Bible Story: John 13:1–20, Jesus Washing the Disciples' Feet

Storyteller: Peter and/or John talking about Jesus washing their feet the night before Jesus died. Jesus served them instead of putting them down or being unkind.

Promise Path Memory Verse: I did this as an example for you. So you should do as I have done for you. John 13:15 (ICB) (all children)

OPTIONAL SESSION 3

Promise Path Action Topic: Promise Kids Get Involved at Church

Bible Story: Exodus 35:20–29; 36:2–7, The Furnishing of the Tabernacle

Storyteller: One of the Israelites who got involved with building and furnishing the Tabernacle

Promise Path Memory Verse: God has shown you his grace in giving you different gifts. . . . So be good servants and use your gifts to serve each other. 1 Peter 4:10 (ICB)(all children)

OPTIONAL SESSION 4

Promise Path Action Topic: Promise Kids Accept Others as Jesus Does

Bible Story: Luke 10:25–37, The Good Samaritan

Storyteller: The man who was robbed and beaten telling what it felt like to be ignored, but then finally helped by the Good Samaritan, and how the experience helped him (a Jew) accept someone from a culture he might have been prejudiced toward

Promise Path Memory Verse: Christ accepted you, so you should accept each other. This will bring glory to God. Romans 15:7 (ICB) (older children); Christ accepted you, so you should accept each other. Romans 15:7 (ICB)(younger children)

OPTIONAL SESSION 5

Promise Path Action Topic: Promise Kids Make a Difference in Their World

Bible Story: John 6:1–15, Jesus Feeds Five Thousand

Storyteller: One of Jesus' disciples telling about the boy who came forward to share his lunch with others, emphasizing what children today can do for the needy of this world

Promise Path Memory Verse: Jesus said to the followers, "Go everywhere in the world. Tell the Good News to everyone." Mark 16:15 (ICB) (older children); Tell the Good News to everyone. Mark 16:15 (ICB) (younger children)

SUGGESTED LIFE APPLICATION PROJECTS AND ACTIVITIES

These projects are organized by age range, with the easiest ones first. With help, the younger children can be successful with most of these projects.

1. Promise Path Puzzle
Goal: Participants will create a Promise Path puzzle to help them review the 50-Day Adventure.

Length: This project will take approximately one week to complete and is best for children in grades K–2. It requires minimal preparation, cleanup, and storage.

Supplies: Construction paper, scissors, markers, pens, clear contact paper

Directions:
• Write one of the Promise Path Action Topics onto a piece of construction paper. Then write down different ways to carry out that promise. Decorate as desired.
• Use a marker to create puzzle pieces out of the paper. Divide it into easy-to-cut-out sections, avoiding tiny ends and corners. Younger children should divide the paper into no more than five or six sections. Older children should keep it to ten or twelve pieces.
• Cover the puzzle with contact paper and then cut on the marked lines.

• Mix up the pieces and reassemble to review.

Questions: Ask these questions as the children are working: **What can be puzzling about following God's directions? Do we always have the answers for doing what Jesus would do? How can following God's directions help put the pieces of our life's problems together?**

2. Promise Path Pinwheels

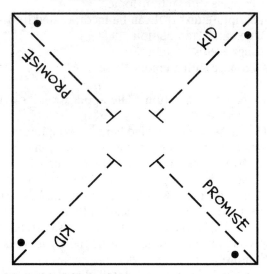

Goal: Participants will create a pinwheel to proclaim they are a Promise Kid.

Length: This project will take one week to complete and is best for children in grades K–2. It requires minimal preparation, cleanup, and storage.

Supplies: Colorful paper, scissors, pinwheel pattern, markers, tape, 1/2" diameter wooden dowel, hammer, 1/4" nail, stapler

Directions:
• Enlarge and photocopy the pinwheel pattern onto colorful cardstock on a photocopy machine, one for each child.
• Cut out the square and decorate as desired, using markers.
• Cut on each dotted line. Then fold the corner of the dotted section into the center of the square and staple in place.
• Punch a 1/4" nail through the center of the pinwheel and hammer it into a 1/2" wooden dowel. Adults should do this part. Leave enough room for the pinwheel to spin.
• Place in a location to proclaim that you are a Promise Kid!

Questions: Ask these questions as the children work: **What do you think it means to be a Promise Kid? Where does your Promise Path lead? Why do we have to follow God's directions while staying on the Promise Path? How can we stay on the Promise Path?**

3. Promise Path Pennants or Flags

Goal: Participants will create Promise Path pennants to proclaim the acceptance of others. This correlates with the topic in Week 6.

Length: This project will take one to two weeks to complete and can be used for all ages. It requires minimal preparation, cleanup, and storage.

Supplies: Felt, yardstick, scissors, glue, markers, paper, pencils, dowel rod (for flags)

Directions:
• Cut a 10" x 20" piece of felt to use as the pennant background, or a 20" x 30" piece of felt to create a flag.
• For flags, fold over two inches of felt along the left side. Spread glue on 1/2" of the edge and press in place. Let dry. Use this loop to slip a dowel rod into. (See diagram.)
• For pennants, attach two 1" x 3" strips of felt to the upper and lower portion of the 10" side. (See diagram.)
• Ask kids to think of slogans of acceptance to put onto their pennants or flags. For example: "I Accept You, Yes I Do!"
• Write and draw sample designs onto a piece of paper, using the slogans they created.
• Tell kids to transfer their design onto the pennant or flag by using pieces of felt and/or markers.

Questions: Ask these questions, or similar ones, as the kids work: **How does it feel to not be accepted? To be accepted? How can we show our acceptance of others? Why is it important to accept others like Jesus does?**

4. Promise Path Plaque

Goal: Participants will create a Promise Path plaque as a reminder of the PURITY acronym learned with the topic "Do What Jesus Would Do."

Length: This project will take approximately two weeks to complete. It can be done by all ages, but the younger children will need help. It requires minimal preparation, but a little extra cleanup and storage.

Supplies: Tongue depressors, glue, wide ribbon, pens, wood stain, brushes, magnetic tape

Directions:
• Cut a 13" strip of wide decorative ribbon. Cut an upside-down *V* out of one end to create points. Lay the ribbon on a flat surface.
• Write the following PURITY acronym onto seven tongue depressors with a pen:

1. P-U-R-I-T-Y

2. Put away put-downs

3. Undo unkind actions

4. Run from things you know are wrong

5. Invite an adult who loves you to help you

6. Think God's thoughts

7. Yell for joy and high-five whenever you do what Jesus would do.

• Spread wood stain onto each tongue depressor with a brush. Let dry.
• Glue each tongue depressor onto the center of the wide ribbon, leaving one inch of ribbon in between each one.
• Attach a piece of magnetic tape onto the back of the top tongue depressor to cling to the refrigerator.

Questions: Ask these questions, or ones that are similar, as the children work: **How can we put away put-downs and encourage others to do it too? How can we undo unkind actions? How can we run away from things we know are wrong? What adults can we invite to help us with problems? What kind of thoughts are godly thoughts? Why yell and high-five when we follow God's directions?**

5. Promise Path Pals

Goal: Participants will make Promise Path play pals to help them remember one Promise Path Action Topic in the 50-Day Adventure.

Length: This project will take approximately two to three weeks to complete and is best for older children (grades 2—6). It requires minimal preparation, cleanup, and storage.

Supplies: Yarn; scissors; plastic needles; 8" x 3" piece of sturdy cardboard; plain light-colored fabric; pen

Directions:
• To form the Promise Path pal's body, wrap yarn around an 8" length of the cardboard approximately 75 times.
• Cut a 6" piece of yarn and weave it between the cardboard and the wrapped yarn. Pull the piece together and tie it securely in place in the center. Then slip the yarn off the cardboard. The tied portion is the front, and the untied portion is the back.
• Create a head by cutting another 6" piece of yarn and wrapping it around the top two inches of the pal. Tie and knot securely in place. Add facial features by using a different color yarn to create knots wherever desired (eyes, nose, mouth) on the front of the face. Cut the ends close to the knot.
• Cut the bottom ends of the yarn on the pal. To make arms, pull half of the back portion of the untied yarn to each side and tie them two inches from the end, creating wrists. Trim 1 1/2" off the hands.
• Leave the bottom portion of the yarn loose to create a skirt, or split it in half to create pants. If making a skirt, tie a belt around the entire waist line at this time. For pants, divide in half and tie each pant leg 1/2" from the bottom to create ankles.
• To make hair, wind another bunch of yarn around a small piece of cardboard (whatever size you desire). The longer your cardboard, the longer the hair will be. The more yarn you wrap around the cardboard, the fuller the hairstyle will be. Tie it together at one end and cut the opposite end. Weave a piece of yarn through the top of the pal's head and use it to tie on the hair. Cut it as desired, make pigtails or a ponytail, or even add a hair bow or ribbon.
• Complete girl pals by cutting an apron out of a plain piece of fabric. Complete boy pals by cutting a bandana out of a plain piece of fabric. Write one of the Promise Path Action Topics onto the apron or bandana with pen. Tie around the pal's waist or neck as a reminder of that promise.

Questions: Ask these questions as the children are working: **Why did you choose this Promise Path Action Topic? Where will you put your Promise Path pal to remind you of a way to follow God's directions? In what ways will you to try to do this?**

6. Promise Path Pouch or Purse

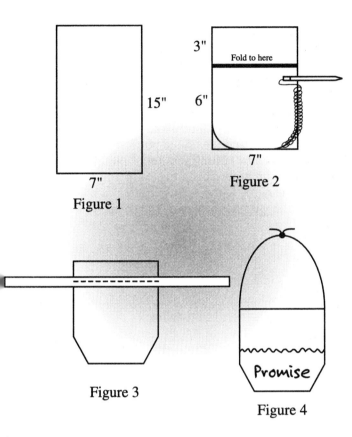

3"
Fold to here
6"
15"
7"

7"
Figure 1

Figure 2

Figure 3

Promise
Figure 4

Goal: Participants will create a purse or pouch as a reminder of their 50-Day Adventure.

Length: This project will take approximately three to four weeks to complete and is best for older children (grades 2–6). It requires minimal preparation, cleanup, and storage.

Supplies: Plain fabric, burlap, plastic needles, embroidery floss, scissors, fabric paint, index cards, pens, pins, velcro tape

Directions:
• Cut a 15" x 7" piece of fabric or burlap. Fabric will create a purse for girls and burlap will make a pouch for boys.
• Fold 6" of fabric up from the bottom. Round both bottom corners and cut out.
• Thread a plastic needle with embroidery floss. Sew the sides of the purse or pouch from the bottom to the top of each side. Older children can do this by first pinning the bottom folded portion in place, sewing a regular stitch, then turning it inside out. Younger children can do this by looping the floss around the outside of the fabric from the bottom to the top of each side. Be sure an adult or older teen supervises.
• Cut a strip of fabric or burlap 1" by whatever length of strap you desire. Center it onto the bottom of the open flap. Sew it in place using a back stitch. Then tie ends of the strap together in a knot.
• Use fabric paint to write the word *Promise* on the outside, and decorate as desired.
• Attach a piece of velcro tape to keep the purse or pouch closed.
• Provide index cards for kids to copy each of the Promise Path Action Topics and/or Promise Path Memory Verses to keep inside their purse or pouch. Use it as a reminder of the 50-Day Adventure and each week's lesson.

Questions: As the children are working ask these questions or ones similar: **What kinds of things do you like to carry around with you wherever you go? Why should we carry around our promises wherever we go? Why is it important to keep our promises? Does God keep his promises to us? How?**

WEEK ONE OVERVIEW

- **Promise Path Action Topic:** Stop and Think About Jesus
- **Desired Outcome:** That the children will learn to take a small amount of time each day to stop and think about Jesus, through prayer, Bible reading, music, quiet time, or other appropriate activities.
- **Bible Story:** Luke 10:38–42
- **Promise Path Memory Verse:** God says, "Be quiet and know that I am God. I will be supreme over all the nations. I will be supreme in the earth." Psalm 46:10 (ICB) (older children); God says, "Be quiet and know that I am God." Psalm 46:10 (ICB) (younger children)
- **Bible Story Presentation:** Story told by Martha
- **Life Application Projects:** The Life Application Projects that relate specifically to the Promise Path Action Topic for Week 1 are Promise Path Prayer Book (p. 92) and Promise Path Sculpture (p. 102).

Getting Started

See "Ready to Begin: Administrative Information" on page 9 for an overview of the children's Adventure program, attendance suggestions, and the selection, identification, and naming of the children's Small Groups. The "Bible Story Time" section on pages 13–16 will provide you with suggestions for how to set up your Promise Path Factory.

As the children arrive, they should stop by the Promise Path check-in table to record their attendance, pick up their color-coded name tags, and meet their Small Group leaders. You might explain that the children are to drop off their name tags at the check-in table when they leave each week.

The first day of the Adventure can be confusing for some children, so allot time for orienting children to the program. If you have chosen to offer Life Application Projects first, explain what is available and where they are located, before you send kids on their way. If you have selected Bible Story Time as your opening activity, be sure to offer an introductory activity, such as singing, as children gather for the presentation.

LIFE APPLICATION PROJECTS

Choose projects appropriate for the age and interests of your children. Refer to "Life Application Projects" (p. 84) and "How Long Do I Spend on Each Part of the Session?" (p. 8). Plan to have one project worktable and one adult leader for every 10–12 children. During Week 1, children will need an opportunity to preview each project before making their initial decision of where to work. Because of the need for introduction, children will not have a chance to accomplish much during the first week. But don't worry; this will give the kids something to look forward to in the following sessions. Since today's topic is "Stop and Think About Jesus," you might suggest that the children begin to work on the Promise Path

Prayer Book and/or the Promise Path Sculpture described on pages 92 and 102.

BIBLE STORY TIME

Have the children gather in a large group and sit with their Small Group leaders. For ideas on how to make Bible Story Time more effective, see pages 13–16.

Weekly Activities

Welcome the children to the 50-Day Adventure. Explain that they have just entered the Promise Path Factory, a place where everyone works on making the things that help us follow God's directions and travel on the Promise Path. Use this time for making announcements, acknowledging birthdays, or taking an offering. If you are using this curriculum for your children's church program, you may prefer to take the offering during worship time.

Setting the Scene

Things You'll Need: Design your Promise Path Factory by building the Conveyor Belt that will produce the weekly Promise Path Memory Verse. You will also need a Bible Time Machine that will help take kids back to Bible times where the weekly story takes place. The Bible Time Machine will also generate the weekly Promise Path Action Topic. Explanations for how to create these items and other suggestions for preparing the Factory are found on pages 13–16 of this leader's guide.

To complete today's topic introduction, you'll need a handmade Stop sign, factory clothes for the leader, and a feather duster or dust cloth.

PREPARATION

To set the stage, try to dress as a factory worker. Bib overalls or bluejeans and a flannel shirt will work nicely.

This week you will also need someone dressed up as Martha, sister of Lazarus and Mary. This person will be hidden inside the Bible Time Machine. Provide her with a copy of the script in the Bible Story Presentation below.

Each week you will challenge the group with a specific way they can learn how to follow God's directions. Print each week's Promise Path Action Topic on a piece of paper large enough for kids to read from a distance. Then place it in the Bible Time Machine for use at the appropriate time.

Today's Promise Path Road Sign is a Stop sign. You will need someone to carry the sign into the Factory and place it in front of the leader at the time indicated.

All of these preparations will make your Factory come alive with the Adventure theme "Promise Kids on the Promise Path"!

TOPIC INTRODUCTION
(Enter Factory singing, preparing for work. Carry a feather duster or a dust cloth and begin dusting the Promise Path Road Signs, Bible Time Machine, Conveyor Belt, and so on. After a moment, look out toward the children and stop what you're doing.)

Oh, hi! Welcome to our 50-Day Spiritual Adventure, "Promise Kids on the Promise Path: Learning How to Follow God's Directions." This is the Promise Path Factory where everyone works on making the things that help us follow God's directions and travel on the Promise Path. I'm really glad you came to work with me today! I'm the factory foreman, which really means I'm your leader. I help the work crews get organized so that we get the job done right.

Let's get to work! Does anyone know what a promise is? (Let kids respond.) **Good answers! A promise is an agreement to do something. In the Promise Path Factory, we make a variety of Promise Path Road Signs that help us think about ways we can follow God's directions.** (Person comes out holding a Stop sign and places it directly in front of the leader. The leader reads it.) **Stop! I was just talking about road signs, and that's a nice one. But not now, okay? I'm busy. I'm talking about important matters to our new work crew.**

Now, as I was saying, in the Promise Path Factory, we work hard thinking about what it takes to follow God's directions. (Person with the Stop sign follows the leader [who is moving energetically around the room] and once again places the sign directly in front of him or her.)

(Leader is straining to be polite.) **That's a great Stop sign, but I'm rather busy right now, okay?** (Back to kids.) **Sorry about that. Where was I? Oh, yes, following God's directions. In the Bible, God has given us all sorts of directions on how to live as his children.** (Once again, the person carrying the Stop sign places the sign in front of the leader.)

(Out of patience.) **Enough with that Stop sign! I've seen it already! What am I supposed to do? Stop what I'm doing?** (Person holding the sign gives an exaggerated nod. Leader looks slightly embarrassed.) **I can't stop now; my work crew is waiting for me! And I'm trying to explain about God's directions. God doesn't tell us to STOP anywhere in the Bible, does he?** (Person holding the sign gives another exaggerated nod. Leader frowns and thinks about this for a moment.) **He does?** (Person nods, then brings the leader to the Bible Time Machine.)

This is our Bible Time Machine that helps us go back in time to see what the Bible tells us about following God's directions. I think I'm supposed to stop and see what our Bible Time Machine has for us today. (Leader pulls the Promise Path Action Topic for Week 1 out of the Bible Time Machine mail slot. The person holding the Stop sign looks pleased. After today's topic is produced, the leader holds it up for everyone to read.)

Let's read today's Promise Path Action Topic together. "Stop and think about Jesus." Oh! Now I understand. I was so busy getting ready for today's work, I forgot the most important reason we're here! Has that ever happened to you? (Let kids respond.) **That's why today's topic is so important. It reminds us to take some time each day and think about Jesus. Jesus doesn't want us to get so busy with everything else that we forget to stop and think about him! What an important reminder. What kinds of things are you busy with during the week?** (Let kids name a few things that keep them busy, like school work, chores, playing with friends, TV, and so on.) **I get busy with a lot of things, too! But no matter how busy we get, we should never forget to stop and think about Jesus every day!**

You know what? From now on, whenever I see a Stop sign, I think I'll remember to stop and think about Jesus!

Let's go to our Promise Path Factory Time Machine that can take us back to Bible times to see how people living then stopped to think about Jesus! (Invite someone to join you in cranking up the Bible Time Machine that will produce today's storyteller.)

Bible Story Presentation

Bible Basis: Luke 10:38–42
Storyteller: Martha

Things You'll Need: Traditional Bible-time clothes for "Martha" underneath an apron and a chef's hat. She may use the feather duster from "Setting the Scene" as a prop. Set a small table in the imaginary kitchen stage right, and plan for the door to Martha's home to be stage left. A plate or bowl (made of pottery, if possible) and cloth napkin should be on the table.

Martha: *(relaxed, happily dusting everthing she sees—even children—with the feather duster)* I could hardly wait for Jesus to arrive. Just think! He was coming back to our home in Bethany for a visit. "Martha," my older brother, Lazarus, said to me, "we've got to get this house spic-and-span! It's not every day that we have the Son of God come to dinner!"

(She sets the feather duster down on the floor, arranges the plate or bowl in a suitable spot on the table, and folds the napkin as she talks.)

Lazarus and my younger sister, Mary, and I hurried to get the house ready and the food brought home from the market. And when at last the table was nearly set, the quail was roasting, and rice was cooking (though I hadn't started the vegetables yet), Jesus—and a *lot* of people who traveled with him—came to our door.

(Martha somewhat nervously acts out the scene, rushing over to "door" and kissing an imaginary Jesus first on the right cheek, then on the left cheek, then again on the right cheek in typical Middle Eastern fashion. Everything she does is quick and a little distracted.)

"Peace, Jesus! Welcome to our home! Peace to you all—Peter, Andrew, James, John, Philip, Thomas, Matthew, James, Thaddaeus, Simon, Judas, Bartholomew . . . oh, dear."

(Martha runs to the kitchen, calling out as she goes.)

"Lazarus, see that everyone is comfortable. Mary, there's lots to do! Jesus, I'm afraid you'll all have to talk for a little while—dinner isn't quite ready!"

(turning back to the audience) I started to work with the quail, rice, and vegetables—oh, let's see—I needed someone to run to the neighbor's to borrow some extra serving platters. Where was Mary? She could help. Where was she? *(Martha looks around.)* She wasn't in the kitchen. Oh, great! On top of a huge meal to prepare and serve, I would have to find a lost sister!

(looking around the kitchen area, then crossing over to center stage—the "great room") I searched everywhere, inside and outside, until at last I reached the great room where all our guests were seated. No, she wasn't taking care of the twelve men's coats and shoes. There she was, seated on the floor, right beside Jesus!

"Mary," I cried, "what are you doing?" She didn't say anything; I don't think she even heard me. I knew my sister Mary. She was so busy paying attention to Jesus she didn't even know there were other people around! If I was going to get any help, I'd have to talk to Jesus himself about it.

So I went over to him and asked, "Lord, don't you care that my sister has left me to do the work by myself? Tell her to help me!"

Jesus looked at me, and his eyes were smiling as he said to me ever so gently: "Martha, Martha, you are worried and upset about many things. But only one thing is important." Jesus was so nice to me that I felt like crying—oh, he loves us so much! But he went on: "Mary has chosen to do what is most important. I'm not going to take that away from her."

I knew what that "most important" thing was. It was *him*—Jesus. He was kindly reminding me that time with people—and most of all with God himself—is more important than fancy dinners and comfortable surroundings.

(Martha sits down on the floor.)

The roast quail was kind of burned. The rice was a little mushy, and the vegetables weren't quite done. But I didn't worry about it anymore. We had plenty to eat, and we all enjoyed one another's company. And even better, I got to spend time with Jesus— *(looking up as if at Jesus)* sat on the floor right next to him, just like Mary.

(looking back at the audience) So? I'm not the perfect hostess. Other things are more important. I'm glad I worked hard for Jesus before he (and *so* many followers!) arrived. But I'm also glad I stopped thinking about my own work and paid attention to the one who is most important.

Comprehension Questions

Briefly discuss these questions with the children to clarify the main ideas in the Bible Story Presentation.

• **Why was Martha so busy?** (Jesus, a very important guest, was coming to dinner; Martha didn't expect the disciples to come, too; she had a lot of cooking and cleaning to do; etc.)

• **What was Mary doing?** (sitting and paying attention to Jesus)

• **What did Martha learn after talking to Jesus?** (paying attention to Jesus was most important, she didn't have to worry if the meal didn't turn out just right, etc.)

Promise Path Memory Verse

Things You'll Need: Stop sign, Promise Path Memory Verse (Psalm 46:10) written on the Conveyor Belt scroll. You will also need to write each word of today's Promise Path Memory Verse on a separate index card. Then hide the cards in various locations around your Promise Path Factory.

Each week the children will have an opportunity to learn a new Promise Path Memory Verse.

What a great Conveyor Belt! It produces Promise Path Memory Verses that teach us how to follow God's directions. Every factory should have a conveyor belt like ours, don't you think? I'm so glad we got a chance to meet Martha and hear how she learned to stop and think about Jesus and pay attention to him. Let's crank up the Conveyor Belt and see if we can produce a Promise Path Memory Verse for today. Would someone in my new work crew come up to help me? (Invite a child to come up and crank the Conveyor Belt with you until this week's Promise Path Memory Verse is in full view of your audience.)

Thanks. Let's read it together. "God says, 'Be quiet, and know that I am God. I will be supreme over all the nations. I will be supreme in the earth.'"

Why do you think the verse tells us to be quiet? (Let the kids respond.) **Sometimes, being quiet means no talking. Or sometimes it means listening, like you're doing right now. If we are talking all of the time, how can we ever listen to what God might be trying to tell us? We can also be quiet by resting our bodies and minds from all of our regular, busy work. Then we have time to focus on God.**

The verse also talks about God's being supreme over all nations and over all the earth. When do you think God showed that he is supreme over all the earth? (At creation, the Flood, parting the Red Sea, raising Jesus from the dead, etc.) **God created the entire world. And when God sent us his son, Jesus, he showed us just how much he loves the earth and the people he created! That's why it's so important to stop and think about Jesus. God sent Jesus to be our Savior. He died for us so that our sins are forgiven and to give us new life with him forever! That's a good reason to be quiet and know that he is God!**

Our last job today in the Promise Path Factory is to play a game that will help us to remember today's Promise Path Memory Verse. I need several volunteers for this game. (Choose five or six volunteers.) **Each word of today's verse has been** hidden somewhere in the Promise Path Factory, **and it's your job to walk around and find them. The job for the rest of us is to decide when our searchers need to STOP and think about what they're doing. Each time the audience whispers "STOP!" I'll hold up the Stop sign. Then the searchers must stop and be very quiet while I give a clue by pointing toward a place where one of the words is hidden. We'll keep going until all of the words have been found. Ready? Begin!**

If you choose to have the younger children learn a shorter version of the verse—"Be quiet and know that I am God." Psalm 46:10—you can split them off from the group during the Promise Path Memory Verse presentation. Another option is to have the Small Group leaders work on the verse when they meet with the children (if the Small Groups are age-graded).

LIFE APPLICATION SMALL GROUP TIME

For instructions on working with the Small Groups, see "Tips for Small Group Leaders" on page 21 and the Life Application section under "Ready to Begin: Weekly Leader Information" on page 16. Small Group leaders will need a copy of the Life Application pages (34–35) to lead their groups this week. They will need these pages at least one week ahead of time.

Each Small Group leader will need to make a poster of the Promise Kids Prayer, which can be found on page 21. The leader might enlist the help of his or her Small Group members to make the poster.

CHILDREN'S CHURCH WORSHIP

Things You'll Need: *Promise Kids Sing-along* cassette, audiocassette player, and an offering basket.

If you are using this section, be sure to allow kids a short time to stand up and stretch in between activities. You might also want to include some active songs during the singing time.

Singing

Choose music that fits the theme of this week's Promise Path Action Topic: Stop and Think about Jesus. To reinforce this week's Promise Path Memory Verse, teach the song "Be Quiet and Know That I Am God" on page 105 of this leader's guide. The song can be found on the *Promise Kids Sing-along* cassette. (See p. 128 for ordering information.)

Critter County Story

Through the familiar and friendly Critter County characters, the children can see this week's theme in action and be motivated to stop and think about Jesus. This week's story begins on page 33.

Offering

One way children can learn to worship and respond to God is by giving. If you are using this curriculum for a children's church program, you may prefer to take the offering now instead of during the Weekly Activities portion of the Bible Story Time. Encourage children to stop and think about Jesus as they thank God for something, either verbally or silently, when they pass the offering basket.

Praise and Prayer

Talking to God is the best way to communicate what we feel, need, are thankful for, and want help with. Because children may feel nervous about praying out loud, they will need help and guidance in how to do this comfortably. Remind everyone that there are no "right" or "wrong" things to say to God. He listens to everything we say and always knows just what we mean when we say it.

Each week when you pray together, you will gradually be shifting more of the prayer responsibility from you to the children. You could offer a few sentence prayers, and have the children say a simple response each time. Use a prayer such as the following:

Leader: Lord, we need your help to remember to stop and think about Jesus. Help us, Lord.
Children: Help us, Lord.
Leader: Thank you for helping us learn how to follow your directions. Thank you, Lord.
Children: Thank you, Lord.
All: Amen.

MIDWEEK EXTRAS

Things You'll Need: *Promise Kids Sing-along* cassette, audiocassette player, paper footsteps.

If you are using this curriculum for a midweek children's program or as a combined church school/children's church program during the 50-Day Spiritual Adventure, you may wish to add these fun activities to your time together.

Game
STOP AND THINK ABOUT JESUS!

Things You'll Need: *Promise Kids Sing-along* cassette, audiocassette player, paper footsteps taped on the ground in a large circle.

Have each child stand on a paper footstep (previously created). Play the *Promise Kids Sing-along* cassette as children march to the music. When the music stops, everyone turns to a partner and says, "Stop and think about Jesus!" That person must then say something that helps him or her think about Jesus, such as praying, reading the Bible, listening to a Bible story, thinking about God's love, enjoying the things God created, going to church, and so on. Partners unable to come up with something must sit out the next round, giving them time to stop and think about Jesus. Play continues as long as desired.

The object is to try to think of as many new reasons and ways to stop and think about Jesus as possible!

ADJUSTMENT FOR YOUNGER AGES
Suggest that older and younger children work together as partners. The younger child can have the job of saying "Stop and think about Jesus!" while the older child must come up with the reason or way to think about him.

Singing

Singing is a fun way to praise God. Make use of the songs included in this book, beginning on page 00. Be sure to learn the song *"Be Quiet and Know That I Am God"* on page 105 of this leader's guide. The song can also be found on the *Promise Kids Sing-along* cassette. And remember to include some active songs to give kids an opportunity to move around.

Critter County Story
FROM TEARS TO SMILES

"Everybody gather together, now; it's time for a Critter County story!" All the critters in Grandmother Mouse's house came running from every room. Stories told by this lovable grandmother are always a treat. And after each story, she exchanges her homemade chocolate chip cookies for a hug and a smile.

The grandmother cleared her little mouse throat and began to speak. "I need some of you to help me tell our story today. Do I have any volunteers?" She no more had the words out of her mouth when several raised their paws and wings, saying, "Let me do it. I want to help, Grandmother Mouse."

"Now, now, not just yet. I'll tell you when we get to that part," she said with a smile. "First, let me tell you that our story took place many hundreds of years ago, and Jesus was the one telling the story that time. He was traveling with his disciples, and many people were gathered around him.

"As Jesus was speaking, the disciples tried to quiet the children and get them to leave and go home. Jesus didn't like that, and so he invited the little ones to come to him. Why do you think he did that?"

Shugums the little squirrel held up her paw, because she had an answer. "I think Jesus loves children and wants us to be with him," she said with a smile and a fluff of her tail.

"I believe you are absolutely right, Shugums," said Grandmother Mouse. "And what do you think happened?"

Quick as a butterfly kiss, Rascal the raccoon held up his paw. "I think some of the kids went to him and others were afraid and stayed back."

"Yes, my little friend, I believe that is also correct. Why do you think they were afraid?"

"Oh, I guess some of the kids wouldn't know if Jesus really wanted them or not. And some would wonder if they could trust him. But I know that we can trust him," said the furry raccoon with great confidence.

Grandmother Mouse smiled as she patted him on his head. "I agree with you, Rascal. Now, this is the part where I need some of you to help me."

Grandmother Mouse looked at all the paws, claws, and wings that were waving, trying to get her to pick them. "Let's see. Lunchbox, I believe a bold little lion cub like you would have come up to Jesus.

Would you please come up here with me? And Buttons and Boomer, our bug beepers? How about flying up here? And Okey Dokey Donkey, would you please come?"

As quick as a grasshopper jumps in the air, Lunchbox, Buttons, and Boomer went and stood by Grandmother Mouse. Okey Dokey just sat in the back with a sad look on his face. "What's the matter, Okey Dokey?" asked Grandmother Mouse.

"Oh, I wouldn't go up to Jesus," said the little donkey, who had a big tear in his eye.

"Why?" asked Grandmother Mouse as she went and sat down next to him.

"Because Jesus just loves the smart kids and the ones who play sports really well. He doesn't love losers like me. I can't talk real well and my long, droopy ears make me ugly," sobbed the poor little fellow.

Grandmother Mouse leaned over and patted him on the head. "Oh, my friend, I know just how you feel, and so does Jesus. I had many problems when I was growing up because I was so much smaller than all my friends. They would pick on me. And Jesus understands. He felt people didn't understand him, and he was made fun of, too.

"The truth is that Jesus loves you just the way you are. He loves you as much as he loves the smartest kids and the best looking. You are very, very precious to him. In fact, he loves you so much that he is getting ready for you to come to heaven and live with him forever. He's making a place, just for you to be with him because he wants to be with you."

Grandmother Mouse hugged Okey Dokey and walked back to her chair. As she sat down, she was surprised to turn and see that Okey Dokey had followed her. "Well, have you decided you want to stay close to Jesus?" she asked.

Okey wiped the tears from his eyes with his long, droopy ears. "Yes, I believe Jesus loves me. I didn't know he's making a place for me in heaven! He wouldn't do that if he didn't want me to come and be with him. Can we sing a song, Grandmother Mouse?"

"We sure can." When she started singing, everyone sang with her. "Jesus loves me, this I know, for the Bible tells me so. . . ."

After the song, everyone gathered around to give Okey lots of hugs. Several of the critters told him that they liked him and that he was a best friend! Then they all shared cookies, hugs, and smiles.

LIFE APPLICATION PAGE

For Small Group Leaders
• WEEK ONE •

- **Promise Path Action Topic:** Stop and Think About Jesus
- **Desired Outcome:** That the children will learn to take a small amount of time each day to stop and think about Jesus, through prayer, Bible reading, music, quiet time, or other appropriate activities.
- **Bible Story:** Luke 10:38–42
- **Promise Path Memory Verse:** God says, "Be quiet and know that I am God. I will be supreme over all the nations. I will be supreme in the earth." Psalm 46:10 (ICB) (older children); God says, "Be quiet and know that I am God." Psalm 46:10 (ICB) (younger children)

THINGS YOU'LL NEED

- Copy of "Tips for Small Group Leaders" (p. 21)
- *Bug Beepers for Promise Keepers* Critter County Activity Book (K–2)
- *Promise Kids on the Promise Path* Children's Journal (3–6)
- Promise Kids Prayer Poster
- Promise Path Action Topic Poster (see below)
- Newsprint
- Markers
- Chalkboard and chalk

IN ADVANCE

Make a Promise Path Poster of the Promise Kids Prayer found on page 21. You may also wish to make a poster with a picture of your church (see p. 17). Write each week's Promise Path Action Topic on a path leading from the church. It will make a great room display and serve as a good reminder of each week's focus.

GROUP-BUILDING ACTIVITY

If time permits, do the following group-building activity. Begin by encouraging everyone to share something about themselves with the group. (Kids could share their favorite food, pet, school subject, and so on.) This is an excellent way for the kids to begin forming relationships and start caring for one another. As the group becomes more comfortable with each other, children will be encouraged to pray for each other, too.

Next, ask the children to share a promise they made to someone else or that someone else made to them. Find out if the promise was kept or broken and what that felt like. Be sure that everyone feels comfortable with what they are sharing. Never ask children to share something they feel uneasy about revealing. This is a great activity to get kids thinking about the importance of keeping promises and living like Promise Kids!

KID TALK

The purpose of Small Group Time is to pave the way for children to think and talk about today's Bible story. It is also an excellent way for children to build relationships with an adult who follows God's directions and with other young people within your church. They will share ways to take the message home and talk about how it will affect their lives. Have this week's Promise Path Action Topic displayed on one of the paths coming from the picture of your church on the poster. Encourage kids to do the talking. Ask questions like those listed below. Be prepared to share your own examples to get the discussion moving, but make sure to let the kids do most of the talking.

- **Let's read our Promise Path Action Topic together: Stop and think about Jesus. To get us started, let's make a list of some ways you can stop and think about Jesus.** (Let kids brainstorm as you list their ideas on the chalkboard. Answers might include: by going to a quiet place where you can be alone to think about him; by praying; by reading your Bible; by listening to stories about God; by enjoying God's creation; by listening to Christian music, and so on.)
- **Who was our storyteller in today's Bible story?** (Martha)
- **Why do you think it was important for Martha to stop and pay attention to Jesus?** (Jesus is more important than anything else, she could learn about God, she could find out how much Jesus loved her.)
- **What can you do to be like Martha in today's story?** (Take time to stop and think about Jesus every day.)

• **How will you stop and think about Jesus this week?** (Encourage kids to name specific times and ways they will stop to think about Jesus. Perhaps it will be while they are working on their Adventure journal. Maybe it will be during mealtime and bedtime prayers.)

• **How does today's Promise Path Action Topic, to stop and think about Jesus, help us learn how to follow God's directions?** (We need to take time out to think about Jesus, or we'll never have opportunities to learn about how God wants us to live!)

Show sample copies of the Adventure journals and ask which kids have journals at home. (See the "Small Group Tip" following "Prayer Talk.") Explain that as they follow their journals this week, they'll have more fun learning about this week's Promise Path Action Topic and Promise Path Memory Verse that they discovered today. If the children need the *Promise Kids on the Promise Path* Journal or the *Bug Beepers for Promise Keepers* Critter County Activity Book, consult the order form on page 128. Explain that each week you'll give them a chance to tell each other something about what they're doing in their journals.

PRAYER TALK

Talking to Jesus is a terrific way to let him know we're stopping to think about him every day! It shows we are listening, learning, trusting, and trying to care for one another.

Call attention to your Promise Kids Prayer Poster at this time. (If time allows, you might let your group make the poster rather than making it yourself ahead of time.) **If you have an Adventure journal at home, you're probably familiar with this prayer.**

Read the prayer to the children, or read it together, depending on your age-group. Encourage kids to use the prayer throughout the week as a starting point for spending time with Jesus and talking to God during the 50-Day Spiritual Adventure.

God wants us to spend time with him every day. He wants to hear our problems and concerns as well as our joys and successes! He wants to share everything with us all the time.

Begin the prayer yourself. Then encourage children to talk to Jesus in their own words. They may wish to extend a word of thanks, ask for help or forgiveness, celebrate something good or special, or pray for someone in need.

SMALL GROUP TIP

The kids in your group have the option of taking part in the 50-Day Spiritual Adventure on a daily basis by using a journal. The journal for grades 3–6 is called *Promise Kids on the Promise Path*. The activity book for preschool–grade 2 is called *Bug Beepers for Promise Keepers*. Although the kids do not need to bring these books to church, they will get a lot more out of the Adventure if they do the daily activities at home. The topics and memory verses are the same as those the kids learn at church in the weekly sessions.

During Small Group Time each week, you will be asked to talk with the kids about what they're learning in their journals. This will help children keep track of how well they are applying the truths they learn to their lives. Since some of the children may not have their own journals yet, you'll need to check with their parents or your church's Adventure coordinator about getting them copies.

WEEK TWO OVERVIEW

- **Promise Path Action Topic:** Find Friends Who Help You Follow Jesus
- **Desired Outcome:** That children will make an effort to find a friend who can help them follow Jesus. During the Adventure, this might mean finding a friend to check up on what they're learning in their Adventure Journal or Activity Book at home.
- **Bible Story:** Romans 1:1–12; 16:1–19
- **Promise Path Memory Verse:** A good person takes advice from his friends. But an evil person is easily led to do wrong. Proverbs 12:26 (ICB) (all children)
- **Bible Story Presentation:** Story told by Paul
- **Life Application Project:** The Life Application Project that goes well with the Promise Path Action Topic for Week 2 is "Friendship Bracelets or Medallions" (p. 90)

Getting Started

As the children arrive, have them check in at the Adventure table, pick up their color-coded name tags, and meet their Small Group leaders. They can then proceed to work on the Life Application Project of their choice or move to the Bible Story Time with their Small Group leaders.

LIFE APPLICATION PROJECTS

Continue to offer ongoing projects, adding new ones as your schedule permits. (You can find more detailed information on pp. 84–104 on how to set up and work with the projects.) Consider any new projects that correlate with this week's lesson as noted in the Overview. That project will help kids experience an activity that promotes finding friends who help them follow Jesus.

BIBLE STORY TIME

Gather the children together in a large group. They can sit within their Small Group families.

Weekly Activities

Welcome the children back to the Adventure. Proceed by making any necessary announcements, recognizing birthdays, or taking an offering.

Setting the Scene

Things You'll Need: Promise Path Factory Bible Time Machine with this week's Promise Path Action Topic, Conveyor Belt with this week's Promise Path Memory Verse, a Pedestrian Crossing sign, and an orange vest or crossing guard belt (if possible). This week you will also need two or three children's riding vehicles—such as a tricycle or other scooter car—and masking tape.

Preparation

Dress as a crossing guard today. An orange vest or crossing guard belt over your normal clothing will be fine. You will also need someone dressed up as Paul for this week's Bible story. This person will be hidden inside the Bible Time Machine. Provide a copy of the monologue in the Bible Story Presentation below.

Write this week's Promise Path Action Topic on a piece of paper large enough for kids to read. Then put it into the Factory's Bible Time Machine for use at the appropriate time. Today's Promise Path Road Sign is the Pedestrian Crossing sign.

Make a Promise Path roadway for kids to ride the toy vehicles on. You can do this by creating a narrow road in the shape of a circle, using masking tape on the floor.

Topic Introduction

(Enter the Factory dressed as a crossing guard. You will need several volunteers for your Pedestrian Crossing path. Two or three kids need to hop onto the available toy riding vehicles. Another two volunteers will try to cross the road the vehicles are traveling on.)

Good morning! Welcome back to the Promise Path Factory where we're learning how to be Promise Kids who follow God's directions. Today I'd like to do an experiment, and I'll need about four or five volunteers. (Get volunteers at this time and tell them what to do. Ask the drivers to start circling the path after you, and ask the other volunteers to stand inside the pathway circle. Tell drivers to obey any signals given by the crossing guard as they drive. Be sure to caution the drivers to ride carefully and avoid collisions.)

Today I'm wearing a crossing guard vest/belt. What's the job of a crossing guard? (Let kids respond.) **Crossing guards help people called pedestrians cross the road safely. Today we have a real Promise Path road, and look at our drivers go! I sure hope they'll travel carefully.**

As our drivers continue to circle the Promise Path in our Factory, we need to decide how pedestrians are going to get across the path. Does anyone have any ideas? (Let kids respond.)

As a crossing guard, I need to help these pedestrians get safely to the other side of the path so that they can return to their seats. (Hold up your Pedestrian Crossing sign as you step out into the path. Drivers should come to a halt. After they do, motion for pedestrians to cross the path safely and return to their seats.)

Whew! They made it to the other side safe and sound! Thanks for your help, volunteers. But what does this have to do with living like Promise Kids? Let's see if our Bible Time Machine can help us out. (Go to the Time Machine and pull out this week's Promise Path Action Topic.) Today's Promise Path Action Topic is to "find friends who help you follow Jesus." Why do you think it's important for us to find friends who will help us follow Jesus? (Let kids respond.) Other Christian friends will want to follow God's directions, just like we do!

What could have happened if there had been no crossing guard or Pedestrian Crossing sign on our Promise Path road today? (Allow time for responses.) Our pedestrians might have collided with cars, and that would have led to big trouble. The same thing can happen when none of our friends want to follow God's directions. We could end up in big trouble! What kinds of things might people do who don't help us follow Jesus? (Let kids respond. Answers might include lying, stealing, cheating, and so on.)

Today's story is about a man named Paul. Paul had many Christian friends because he knew how important it was to help one another follow God's directions. Let's turn on our Time Machine and go back to Bible times so we can all meet Paul.

Bible Story Presentation
Bible Basis: Romans 1:1–12; 16:1–19
Storyteller: Paul

Things You'll Need: A Bible-time costume for Paul; a map of Paul's missionary journeys (may be an enlarged photocopy from the back of a Bible or Bible dictionary) mounted on poster board and set up on an easel or chalkboard.

Today's story is a monologue by Paul. Paul, also known as Saul, persecuted Christians before his con-version experience (Acts 9). He was introduced to Christians in Jerusalem by Barnabas and spent the remainder of his life dedicated to the ministry of spreading the Good News by establishing new churches and then building them up.

Paul: (*Speak while setting up the map.*) Grace and peace to you from God our Father and from the Lord Jesus Christ! My name is Paul, and I often greet my friends in Christ like this. It's my way of wishing you all good things in the name of the Lord. Now I want each of you to greet those around you. (*Encourage the children to shake hands and say, "Grace and peace from God."*)

Serving the Lord is my mission. I had many Christian friends in different cities as I worked to spread the Good News about Jesus. I often wrote to my friends in these different churches so we could continue our friendship and help each other follow Jesus while I was traveling my Promise Path all around the world. (*Point to the map.*)

You are my friends in Jesus Christ, too! We all believe that God sent his Son, Jesus, to die for our sins. When we believe in Jesus as our Savior, our sins are forgiven and someday we will live with him forever.

Friends can learn from each other. They can encourage one another. They can love and care for each other. Our friendships are important if we are to stay on the Promise Path and learn to follow God's directions! Our friendships help us fight sin, help to make us wise, and help our faith to grow. As I wrote to my friends in the city of Rome, "Your faith will help me, and my faith will help you" (Romans 1:12). That's the way Christian friendships work!

Let me tell you about some Christian friends who helped me along my Promise Path. (*Point to Jerusalem on the map.*) My friend Barnabas introduced me to Christians in Jerusalem and helped me escape when my life was in danger. My friend Silas went with me on my second missionary trip to spread the Good News of Jesus. (*Point out the path of Paul's second missions trip.*) We traveled all over telling others about Jesus, and we made many new friends. We helped each other through many hard times—in fact, we spent one night in a prison singing praises to God and even went through an earthquake together!

Priscilla and her husband, Aquila, worked with me at making tents while we were telling the story of Jesus to people in Corinth. (*Point to Corinth.*) These friends invited Christians to meet in their home so they could teach them about Jesus. And they even risked their lives for me—that's friendship!

My dear friend Epenetus was the first person to believe in Jesus in the whole province of Asia.

(Point to Asia Minor.) What an exciting time that was! I could go on and on! Do you feel happy about some of your friends who know Jesus? (Allow one or two children to tell about their friends.)

Friends who follow Jesus are so important. They understand what it's like to feel the joy that God can bring into our lives. They understand how we feel when we have trouble deciding what God would want us to do. They can help us make good choices and encourage us to stop and think about Jesus every day.

And they also help us in another way. I remember once I had to confront my friend Peter, who was one of Jesus' disciples. He was doing something that made others feel bad, so I had to let him know the way he was acting was wrong. He took it real well, though! When we do something wrong or make a bad choice, friends can help us get back on the Promise Path and follow God's directions. That's what friends are for!

We have to watch out for people who try to lead us down the wrong path and away from God. Just think—what if I had been stuck around here (point to Jerusalem and Arabia) and never followed God's path for me? Then the many, many people up here (point to Rome, Greece, and Asia Minor) would never have heard about Jesus. And maybe the Good News about the Son of God would never have spread all around the world! When it comes to sharing our faith with those who don't know Jesus, we can remain strong by relying on our Christian friends.

In my letter to the Romans, I wrote, "I want you to be wise in what is good" (Romans 16:19). Does anyone know what that means? (Allow kids to respond.) We have to use the brains God gave us to make smart decisions—ones that will keep us on the Promise Path. And one of the ways we can do that is by finding friends who help us follow Jesus.

Comprehension Questions
Briefly discuss these questions with the children to clarify the main ideas in the Bible Story Presentation.
• **Why did Paul write letters to his friends at churches in different cities?** (He wanted to continue his friendship; they could help each other follow Jesus.)
• **What does helping each other follow Jesus mean?** (It means to encourage, help, support, and teach one another how to live like Promise Kids.)
• **What is so important about having friends who follow Jesus?** (We can learn together, encourage one another, help each other, understand each other's problems, and be strengthened by knowing we are not alone.)

• **What did Paul say we have to watch out for, and why?** (We have to watch out for people who don't follow Jesus when they tempt us to do things that are wrong. By relying on our Christian friends, we can stay on the Promise Path and continue to follow God's directions.)

Promise Path Memory Verse
Things You'll Need: Promise Path Memory Verse (Proverbs 12:26) written on the Conveyor Belt scroll. You will also need cardboard disks 5" round, circle patterns 4" round for children to cut out, pencils, markers, glue or glue sticks, scissors, tape, safety pins, and clear contact paper (optional).

I need a volunteer to help me crank up our Conveyor Belt to see what today's Promise Path Memory Verse is. (Select a volunteer to crank the lever of your Conveyor Belt until today's verse is showing.)

Let's read what it says. "A good person takes advice from his friends. But an evil person is easily led to do wrong." That's just what Paul told us, isn't it? Our Christian friends can help us a lot. But the people who don't follow Jesus can lead us down the wrong path to unwise decisions.

Our last job today in the Promise Path Factory is to create some Promise Path Memory Verse buttons for our friends! I'm going to distribute the supplies you will need to write today's verse onto a piece of paper. Then you'll glue that paper onto a cardboard disc that you can decorate. Attach a safety pin on the back of it with a piece of tape, and you'll have a Promise Path button to share with a friend!

Distribute the materials and ask everyone to create a button to share with a friend. Cover the finished button with clear contact paper, if desired.

You may also wish to split the group in half during the Promise Path Memory Verse presentation. For children who do not know how to read and write well, write the memory verse onto a circle of paper before class and then photocopy it for children to cut out. This week, we have not suggested a shortened version for younger children.

LIFE APPLICATION SMALL GROUP TIME

Dismiss the children with their Small Group leaders, taking care to let the groups farthest away from the meeting area leave first. Each Small Group leader will need a copy of the Life Application page for today (p. 41). Be sure to give the page to leaders at least a week ahead of time so that they can be ready to work with their groups.

CHILDREN'S CHURCH WORSHIP

Things You'll Need: *Promise Kids Sing-along* cassette, audiocasette player, and an offering basket.

If you are using this section, be sure to allow kids a short time to stand up and stretch in between activities. You might also want to include some active songs during the singing time.

Singing
Choose music that fits the theme of this week's Promise Path Action Topic: Find Friends Who Help You Follow Jesus. To reinforce this week's Promise Path Memory Verse, teach the song "Everyone Wins" on page 109 of this leader's guide. The song can be found on the *Promise Kids Sing-along* cassette. (See p. 128 for ordering information.)

Critter County Story
Through the familiar and friendly Critter County characters, the children can see this week's theme in action and be motivated to follow God's directions by finding friends to help them follow Jesus. This week's story begins on page 40.

Offering
One way children can learn to worship and respond to God is by giving. If you are using this curriculum for a children's church program, you may prefer to take the offering now instead of during the Weekly Activities portion of the Bible Story Time. Encourage children to remember their friends that help them follow Jesus as they thank God for something, either verbally or silently, while passing the offering basket.

Praise and Prayer
Continue to help children through a prayer experience by offering them a line and asking them to repeat it. (Refer to Week 1, p. 32.) This week, encourage children to think about one way to find friends to help them follow Jesus. Let the children conclude the prayer time with their own sentences, asking God to help them follow his directions.

MIDWEEK EXTRAS

Things You'll Need: Index cards with letters of the alphabet for each group of four to six children (eliminate the letters: *X* and *Z*.) *Promise Kids Sing-along* cassette, audiocassette player.

Game
FRIENDS HELP YOU FOLLOW JESUS!
Divide kids into groups of four to six each. Place the alphabet cards face down in the middle of each Small Group. Each child takes four cards from the pile and lays them face down. Play begins by a child flipping up his first card and trying to name one way a friend can help him follow Jesus that begins with that letter. For example, the letter *P*—friends can *pray* with or for you; the letter *C*—friends *care* about each other; the letter *H*—friends *help* you make decisions that follow God's directions.

When kids cannot think of something using the letter they have flipped up, they can place it on the bottom of the main deck and flip up another card. When they get to the end of their pile, they begin to draw from the deck. Play continues for as long as desired or until all of the letters have been used.

ADJUSTMENT FOR YOUNGER AGES
Suggest that older children and younger children work together as a team. The younger child can have the job of flipping up the card, and asking, "How can a friend help you follow Jesus using the letter [insert letter]?" The older child comes up with a way to help, using that letter.

Singing
Singing is a fun way to praise God. Make use of the songs included in this book, beginning on page 105. Be sure to learn the song "Everyone Wins" on page 109 of this leader's guide. The song can be found on the *Promise Kids Sing-along* cassette. And remember to include some active songs to give kids an opportunity to move around.

Critter County Story

THE POINT OF THE LESSON

"Hey, c'mon, let's take the shortcut," said Rascal the raccoon to his friend Lunchbox.

"No, we can't do that. We both promised our parents we would always come straight home from school the way they told us," answered the wise little lion cub.

"Oh, you are such a coward. We *are* going straight home from school. We're just going to take a shortcut that will get us there faster! C'mon. Or am I going to have to go without you?" asked Rascal.

"If you go, you'll go without me because I told my parents I would come the way they told me. And, Rascal, I think you should do the same. You promised."

Rascal waved his paw in the air and said, "My parents won't know if you don't tell them." And off he went down the trail to what he thought would be a shortcut home.

Lunchbox had been home over an hour when his mother received a phone call from Rascal's mom. "Lunchbox, Rascal isn't home from school yet, and his mother wants to know if you saw him after school."

Lunchbox was in a tight squeeze. Should he tell the truth and risk having Rascal get angry with him? Or should he say he didn't know anything? Fortunately, he made the right choice and told the truth.

"Mom, tell Rascal's mother that he took the shortcut home. He took the trail behind the Critter County Post Office because he thought he'd beat me home by going that way."

As soon as Rascal's mother heard this, she called her husband at work. Mr. Raccoon immediately left his job and went to look for his son. "Rascal. RASCAL!" he called and called. Within minutes, the bug beepers had heard the news, and they flew into the woods and began looking. They sounded their alarms and flew all around searching for the lost raccoon.

After more than two hours of walking in the woods and calling his son, Rascal's dad finally heard a noise under a sticker bush. The bug beepers flew to the bush and sounded their alarms. "Daddy, is that you?" a faint voice called from under the bush.

Rascal's father rushed over and slowly pulled the tangled little boy out from under the sticker bush. Rascal was covered from head to paws with long, sharp stickers and thorns. His dad started to pull one out. "Ouch!" screamed Rascal.

"We'll have to take you to Dr. Duck and get his help pulling all of these out. It's going to hurt, and I'm so sorry you will have to go through that," said Rascal's daddy.

He picked up his son and began to carry him in his arms as they started home. "Why did you do this, Son? You promised me that you would always come straight home the way your mother and I have taught you. Why did you break your promise?"

Poor little Rascal started to cry because he felt so bad that he had disappointed his father. "I'm so sorry, Dad. I don't know why I broke my promise to you. I thought I could take a shortcut and get home faster. I'm so glad the bug beepers helped you find me because these stickers really hurt," Rascal said as he began to cry even harder.

His daddy held him close and carried him all the way home. Rascal's mom was waiting in the door and gave him a kiss on his face. "Rascal, I am so thankful your father and the bug beepers found you. The next time you are tempted to do something wrong, I hope you'll remember these stickers and how much they hurt. And if your best friend is there trying to help you make a good decision, I hope you will listen to that good advice the next time."

Rascal wiped his tears and said, "I won't break any more promises. These stickers in my arms and legs have cured me once and for all."

Mrs. Raccoon called and made an appointment. Then Mr. Raccoon took his son to see Dr. Duck, who removed each and every sticker. As Rascal left the office, he turned to Dr. Duck and said, "No more broken promises. I got the *point* of this lesson!"

LIFE APPLICATION PAGE

For Small Group Leaders
• WEEK TWO •

- **Promise Path Action Topic:** Find Friends Who Help You Follow Jesus
- **Desired Outcome:** That children will make an effort to find a friend who can help them follow Jesus. During the Adventure, this might mean finding a friend who will check up on what they're learning in their Adventure Journal or Activity Book at home.
- **Bible Story:** Romans 1:1–12; 16:1–19
- **Promise Path Memory Verse:** A good person takes advice from his friends. But an evil person is easily led to do wrong. Proverbs 12:26 (ICB) (all children)

THINGS YOU'LL NEED

- Copy of "Tips for Small Group Leaders" (p. 21)
- *Bug Beepers for Promise Keepers* Critter County Activity Book (K–2)
- *Promise Kids on the Promise Path* Children's Journal (3–6)
- Promise Kids Prayer Poster
- Promise Path Action Topic Poster
- Newsprint
- Markers
- Chalkboard and chalk

KID TALK

This is an important time for children to talk with one another about how they can find friends who help them follow Jesus. It's also a good opportunity to share positive traits about one another and the ways kids already follow Jesus. Use these questions to get the group talking.
• **Let's read our Promise Path Action Topic together: Find friends who help us follow Jesus. To get us started, let's make a list of ways to follow Jesus.** (Let kids brainstorm as you list their ideas on the chalkboard. Answers might include: loving others, caring for one another, teaching others about God, sharing, being helpful, and so on.)
• **What's one reason Paul gave us to have friends who follow Jesus?** (Answers might include: to help one another, to encourage each other, to keep us strong, to help us follow God's directions, and so on.)
• **The action word in today's topic is** *find.* **How do we find friends to help us follow Jesus? Where should we look?** (At church, at home, at school, or in the neighborhood.)
• **Can we also find friends who don't follow Jesus in some of those places?** (Yes.)
• **How do we know whether a friend follows**

Jesus? (We talk about Jesus with one another; we talk about how Jesus helps with our problems, our joys, and our worries; we talk about church or church club; we know the friend follows God's directions.)
• **What's one way you can try to find a friend who follows Jesus this week?** (Let the children state their ideas—there is not one right answer.)
• **Did anyone stop to think about Jesus last week? When did you do it, and how did you do it?** (Let kids share their stories about stopping to think about Jesus. Celebrate the ways they found time to do this. Encourage them to continue this exercise for a few moments each day.)
• **What's one thing you remember from your Journal or Activity Book this week?**

GROUP-BUILDING ACTIVITY
(You may want to do this activity earlier in the session.)

If time permits, do the following group-building activity. Tell kids to write the word "F-R-I-E-N-D" spelled out vertically down a piece of paper. Then have kids find friends who follow Jesus by interviewing one another. During the interviews, kids should ask their friends to share things about themselves. Kids select one item for each person interviewed that begins with one of the letters in the word *friend.* Kids should write that item and the child's name next to that letter in their vertical word. For example:

F riendly Sara
R eally funny Pete
I nteresting Patty
E ntertaining Ron
N ever dull Fred
D ancer Nancy

This is a great activity to help kids get to know one another better and/or find new friends!

PRAYER TALK

When we talk to God today, let's think about finding new friends who help us follow Jesus. Let's begin by praying our Promise Kids Prayer together and finish by telling God one way we decided to find a friend to help us follow Jesus this week!

Using the Promise Kids Prayer Poster, read the prayer together with your group. Encourage kids to finish the prayer by sharing, if they feel comfortable, how they decided to find a friend to help them follow Jesus this week. Be sure to ask the group about any special prayer concerns, requests, or celebrations, and end by praying for each one.

SMALL GROUP TIP

Today's topic is an excellent chance to encourage friendships among your Small Group. The group-building experience is a good way to get to know one another better. Take advantage of that. It will help to strengthen relationships.

Children will open up more with you and with each other as they get to know you better and realize that what they have to say is important.

Record special notes about each child in a journal so that you can have a reflection sheet to refer to before you begin your Small Group Time each week. Children will appreciate that you took the time and effort to remember their special needs. You will build a foundation of trust and friendship and will open the door to meaningful communication.

WEEK THREE OVERVIEW

- **Promise Path Action Topic:** Do What Jesus Would Do
- **Desired Outcome:** That kids will focus on doing what Jesus would do and work with an acronym for the word *purity* during Small Group Time. (See "Desired Outcome" on p. 48.)
- **Bible Story:** Colossians 3:8–9, 12–13
- **Promise Path Memory Verse:** Let us run the race that is before us and never give up. We should remove from our lives anything that would get in the way. And we should remove the sin that so easily catches us. Let us look only to Jesus. Hebrews 12:1–2 (ICB) (older children); We should remove the sin that so easily catches us. Hebrews 12:1 (ICB) (younger children)
- **Bible Story Presentation:** Story told by a Bible-time woman from the church in Colosse.
- **Life Application Projects:** The Life Application Projects that correlate with the Promise Path Action Topic for Week 3 are "Promise Path Key Chains" (p. 88) and "Promise Path Game" (p. 97)

Getting Started

As the children arrive, have them check in at the Adventure table, pick up their color-coded name tags, and meet their Small Group leaders. They can then proceed to work on the Life Application Project of their choice or move to the Bible Story Time with their Small Group leaders.

LIFE APPLICATION PROJECTS

Continue to offer ongoing projects, adding new ones as your schedule permits. (You can find more detailed information on pp. 84–104 on how to set up and work with the projects.) Consider any new projects that correlate with this week's lesson as noted in the Overview. These projects will help kids experience an activity that encourages them to do what Jesus would do.

BIBLE STORY TIME

Gather the children together in a large group. They can sit within their Small Group families.

Weekly Activities

Welcome the children back to the Adventure. Proceed by making any necessary announcements, recognizing birthdays, or taking an offering.

Setting the Scene

Things You'll Need: Promise Path Bible Time Machine with the Promise Path Action Topic for Week 3, Conveyor Belt with this week's Promise Path Memory Verse, factory work clothes, three Stoplight signs, and five index cards (see below).

PREPARATION

Dress as a factory worker today. You will also need someone dressed up as a Bible-time woman from the

church in Colosse for this week's Bible story. This person will be hidden inside the Bible Time Machine. Provide a copy of the monologue in the Bible Story Presentation below.

Write this week's Promise Path Action Topic onto a piece of paper large enough for kids to read. Then put it into the Factory's Time Machine for use at the appropriate time during the session. Today's Promise Path road sign is the Stoplight. You will need to make three stoplights, one with the red light showing brightly, one with the yellow light showing brightly, and one with the green light showing brightly.

Make five index cards with the following situations on them:
1) Bonnie is invited to help out at the Food Pantry this Saturday. It means giving up her free afternoon in order to help the hungry.
2) George is invited to Tim's house after school, along with several other boys. He heard they are planning to shoot off fireworks, which he isn't allowed to do.
3) Betty is shopping with her girlfriend at a department store. They both see a necklace they would love to have, but don't have enough money to buy it.
4) Kurt is way behind in his math homework. His best friend, Pete, is very smart and has already gotten As on all his assignments. Pete left his math folder at Kurt's house after spending the night.
5) Debby's grandmother just got out of the hospital after having surgery. She is going to need some extra help around the house.

TOPIC INTRODUCTION

(Enter the Factory dressed as a worker. You will need five volunteers to read the situations cards you have prepared. You will also need three volunteers to hold up Stoplights.)

Hello! What have you been doing to live like Promise Kids this week? (Allow the children to respond. Affirm their positive reports.)

Let's go right to our Bible Time Machine to

discover today's Promise Path Action Topic. (Go to the Time Machine and pull out the topic.) **Let's read it together. "Do what Jesus would do!" Sounds like really good advice. This morning I need several volunteers to help me with a game so we can try out doing what Jesus would do.** (Pick your volunteers at this time.)

These three volunteers will operate today's sign, the Stoplight! Let's hear it for our stop-lights! (Encourage the audience to applaud.) **When our volunteers read the situation printed on their card, it's going to be your job to "light up" one of these stoplights. You can do that by shouting "Stop!" "Go!" or "Caution!" after listening to each situation. When you shout "Stop!" which color will light up?** (Red. Ask the person holding the red light to raise the light up high.) **When you shout "Go!" which color will light up?** (Green. Ask the person holding the green light to raise the light up high.) **When you shout "Caution!" which color will light up?** (Yellow. Ask the person holding the yellow light to raise the light up high.) **The louder you shout "Stop!" "Go!" or "Caution!" the higher our Stoplights will be raised. Let's see what happens.**

(Ask the first volunteer to read his or her situation. Then ask the audience: "What would Jesus do?" See which light is lit up, then proceed to discuss why the audience feels that way. Continue until all the cards have been read.)

Sometimes it's easy to know what Jesus would do. Other times it's harder, or even unclear. Today's Bible story is about a woman from a church in Colosse. I wonder if they did everything Jesus would do. Let's turn on our Bible Time Machine so we can go back to Bible times and find out. (Turn on the Time Machine until your woman from Colosse enters.)

Bible Story Presentation

Bible Basis: Colossians 3:8–9, 12–13
Storyteller: Woman from Colosse

Things You'll Need: A Bible-time costume for the woman from Colosse, an easel or chalkboard holding the map of Bible lands used last week, a scroll with the title "Letter to the Colossians" written across the top. (This scroll may contain parts of the script for easy line reference.)

Today's story is a monologue by a fictional woman from the church in Colosse, a city in the Roman province of Asia. Although Paul had never been to the church, he wrote to them addressing the false teachings he had heard about in their community.

Woman from Colosse: Hello! Thank you so much for inviting me to your church! I come from a church that was started many years ago during Bible times in a place called Colosse. Colosse is a small city in the Roman province of Asia. (Point to the city on the map.)

I'd like to ask all of you a question before I begin my story. Why do you come to church here in (insert your church's town)? (Let the kids respond.) Those are some of the same reasons I went to the church in Colosse!

My church in Colosse was started by a group of people who believed in Jesus Christ. We wanted to gather together for regular worship, praise, and learning. This was encouraged by many of Jesus' disciples and followers who were trying to spread the Good News after Jesus ~~died~~ went to Heaven.

Did you know that it's our job to keep on telling others about God just as Jesus did when he was here on earth? (Let the children respond.) Each one of us needs to be willing to do our part in spreading the Good News. And do you know what's one way of spreading the Good News? Do what Jesus would do!

It didn't take very long before we started having problems in our church. Some of the people in the church of Colosse started making decisions that *they* thought were right, rather than doing what Jesus would do. Why could that cause problems? (Let the kids respond.) God wants us to do what Jesus would do, even when it's hard or we do not agree.

(Pick up the scroll.) Last week you got to meet a man named Paul. Do you remember him? Paul spent most of his life spreading the Good News about Jesus! When he heard about the problems we were having in the church in Colosse, he decided to write us a very important letter. (Open the scroll and show the children its title.) You can read his letter to us in your Bible. It is in the book called Colossians, which is found in the New Testament. Col. 3:8-17

(From this time on, you may use the scroll as a reference for lines.) Paul was like a very kind father to our church. He didn't spend lots of time scolding us, although some of us deserved it! I suppose Paul knew how hard it is to always do what Jesus would do. So he tried to help us change our ways. He did this by giving us some rules we could follow and teach to others so that we all could do what Jesus would do.

In his letter, Paul asked us to throw away these things in our lives: anger, bad temper, lying, evil words, and doing or saying things that would hurt others. Can someone show me what we look like when we do all these mean things? (Ask two children to *pose in a stance that demonstrates hostility; have them stand to your left.)* Even though *(fill in the children's names)* are looking kind of disagreeable right now, they are actually doing what Jesus would do by helping me out!

And that's what Paul told my church next; he told us to do what Jesus would do—to show love and kindness, humility and gentleness, patience and forgiveness to everybody! Can someone show me what we look like when we do these great things? *(Allow two kids to come up and stand on your right with their arms around each other, showing that they're pals.)* Now, which way of acting do you prefer—this *(indicating right)*, or this *(indicating left)*? I like the people who show love best, and so did Paul. Imagine how it would be if everyone you knew acted that way! There would be a lot fewer problems, that's for sure. *(Dismiss children to their seats with plenty of thanks, especially for the ones who had to be the "bad guys.")*

When I think about everything Paul wrote to us, it really doesn't seem like much to ask. Because doing what Jesus would do fills our lives with joy, happiness, and peace! Sounds pretty good, doesn't it? So even though Paul warned us that we needed to make some changes and work on doing what is right, I'm really glad he wrote us a letter to tell us what to do. Which is why I came to share those things with you!

Do what Jesus would do. It will change your life and help you to experience God's joy and happiness!

Comprehension Questions

Briefly discuss these questions with the children to clarify the main ideas in the Bible Story Presentation.
• **Why did Paul write to the church in Colosse?** (Because he heard they were having some trouble doing what Jesus would do.)
• **What did Paul ask them to stop doing?** (Their sins of anger, bad temper, lying, evil words, and doing or saying things that would hurt others.)
• **What did Paul encourage the people in Colosse to do?** (To do what Jesus would do by showing love and kindness, humility and gentleness, patience and forgiveness to everybody.)

Promise Path Memory Verse

Things You'll Need: You will need Week 3's Promise Path Memory Verse (Hebrews 12:1–2) written on the scroll inside of the Conveyor Belt. You will also need the red light and green light signs from your opening activity.

I need a volunteer to help me crank up our Conveyor Belt to discover today's Promise Path Memory Verse. (Choose a volunteer and crank the lever of your Conveyor Belt until today's verse is showing.)

Let's read what it says. "Let us run the race that is before us and never give up. We should remove from our lives anything that would get in the way. And we should remove the sin that so easily catches us. Let us look only to Jesus." What is the race we are supposed to run? (Let the children respond.) **We are all running the race of life. Who or what is trying to catch us in this race?** (Bad things, temptations, or people who want us to do what is wrong.)

That's just what the woman from Colosse said Paul wrote to them about. He asked them to leave those things behind and instead to look only to Jesus to see what he would do!

Let's finish our time together by playing a game. How many of you have played "Red Light, Green Light"? Today we're going to play a game similar to that. I'm going to use my red and green Stoplight signs as you all line up along the far wall. When I hold up the green light, I will give you a command like "You may move forward by using baby steps." As long as the green light is showing, you can keep going! But if the red light comes up, you must stop! After you stop, try to recite today's Bible verse. If you do a good job, I'll put up the green light and give you another command. If not, you'll have to go back to where you started. (Play the game, giving commands that allow the kids to move slowly forward. Each time you stop, ask them to recite the verse with you as a group. As the group gets better and better, don't ask them to go back as far, or let them inch up a little farther. Continue the game until everyone knows the verse!)

 Younger children can learn the shortened version of the verse—"We should remove the sin that so easily catches us." Hebrews 12:1—if you choose to split the group in half.

LIFE APPLICATION SMALL GROUP TIME

Dismiss the children with their Small Group leaders, taking care to let the groups farthest away from the meeting area leave first. Each Small Group leader will need a copy of the Life Application page for today (p. 48). Be sure to give the page to leaders at least a week ahead of time so that they can be ready to work with their groups.

CHILDREN'S CHURCH WORSHIP

Things You'll Need: *Promise Kids Sing-along* cassette, audiocasette player, and an offering basket.

If you are using this section, be sure to allow kids a short time to stand up and stretch in between activities. You might also want to include some active songs during the singing time.

Singing

Choose music that fits the theme of this week's Promise Path Action Topic: Do What Jesus Would Do. To reinforce this week's Promise Path Memory Verse, teach the song "Remove the Sin" on page 112 of this leader's guide. The song can be found on the *Promise Kids Sing-along* cassette. (See p. 128 for ordering information.)

Critter County Story

Through the familiar and friendly Critter County characters, the children can see this week's theme in action and be motivated to follow God's directions by doing what Jesus would do. This week's story begins on page 47.

Offering

One way children can learn to worship and respond to God is by giving. If you are using this curriculum for a children's church program, you may prefer to take the offering now instead of during the Weekly Activities portion of the Bible Story Time. Encourage children to think about doing what Jesus would do as they thank God for something, either verbally or silently, when they pass the offering basket.

Praise and Prayer

Continue to help children through a prayer experience by offering them a line and asking them to repeat it. (Refer to Week 1, p. 32.) This week, encourage children to think about one way to start doing what Jesus would do during the week. Let the children conclude the prayer time with their own sentences, asking God to help them follow his directions.

MIDWEEK EXTRAS

Things You'll Need: Index cards and pencils, *Promise Kids Sing-along* cassette, audiocassette player

Game
WHAT WOULD JESUS DO RELAY

(Because children will be running or walking fast, depending on your setting, an adult or older teen should give safety instructions and monitor this game.) Divide kids into two groups of five to ten each. Give each person an index card on which to write down a problem or temptation. (You may want to give a couple of examples appropriate to the age of your group.) Team members must compare cards so that no problems are duplicated. Place cards at one end of the room and line up at the opposite end. Each team must race to the opposite team's cards, pick one, read it, and then come up with a solution that would follow what Jesus would do. Finish by reading or telling it to the rest of the group. The first team finished is the winner.

ADJUSTMENT FOR YOUNGER AGES

Suggest that older children and younger children work together as a team. The younger child can have the job of running up to the card and bringing it back to the older partner. Then the partner reads it and they work together to come up with a solution.

If you have only non-readers in your group, prepare the index cards ahead of time by drawing simple sketches of children with problems or temptations. You can also cut out small pictures and glue them on the index cards.

Singing

Singing is a fun way to praise God. Make use of the songs included in this book, beginning on page 105. Be sure to learn the song "Remove the Sin" on page 112 of this leader's guide. The song can be found on the *Promise Kids Sing-along* cassette. And remember to include some active songs to give kids an opportunity to move around.

Critter County Story
WHO'S THE SMARTEST?

"But it's not fair. It's just not fair!" stormed Petunia the skunk as she walked off the soccer field. "Why do you pick all the boys to be on the team? I can play just as well as they can."

Poor Petunia was so upset that she went home and threw herself on her bed and just sobbed. Some of the kids on the playground began to talk about her, saying things like, "She acts like a baby. Why doesn't she grow up?" Then Rascal started to develop an idea to play a mean trick on her.

"I know how we can make her grow up. Tomorrow morning, I'll take her lunch and hide it. Then while we're eating ours, she can just sit and try to figure out where her lunch is. If she figures it out, she can eat it," suggested the naughty raccoon.

Several of his Critter County buddies said things like, "Yeah, let's do it. That'll teach her!"

Just as they were deciding how Rascal would get Petunia's lunch and where he would hide it, Pastor Penguin came strolling by the playground. He stopped for just a minute by the big apple tree and could hear what the kids were planning. He grew very concerned and quietly tried to figure out how to help.

He looked around from behind the tree and saw that the soccer ball was sitting nearby. Nobody saw him pick it up and put it under a bush. Then he walked over to where the kids were talking. "Hey, how's it going?" he asked.

Rascal sat up straight and answered nervously, "Oh, we are fine, most holy, reverend, father, minister, your highness, I mean, Pastor Penguin."

Pastor Penguin cleared his throat. "I have a question for you. I want to test you all to see how smart and grown up you are."

All the critters sat straight up and were so excited. "I love tests like this," said Lunchbox. "I bet I win!"

After everyone settled down, waiting for the question, Pastor Penguin smiled and said, "Okay. The smartest one of you will be able to tell me exactly where the soccer ball is."

Almost everyone waved their paws and wings in the air. "I know, I know!" they all shouted in unison. Each was sure it was right where they had left it—over by the slide.

So Pastor Penguin let them answer and tell him where they thought it was. They were so surprised when they looked around and saw that it wasn't there. "Can anyone tell me where it is?" he asked.

All the critters sat very still because they didn't know where the ball was. "Now this is the test. Does knowing or not knowing where the ball is have anything to do with how smart you are or how grown up you are?"

The kids all looked at each other and said, "No, of course not."

Then Pastor Penguin asked another question, "Does knowing where a lunch is hidden show how smart someone is?" Suddenly, the critters started to figure out the pastor's message. They began to feel very ashamed because of the way they were acting.

"Now I have another test question for you. If Jesus were here with us, how do you think he would treat Petunia?" asked the wise pastor.

Rascal sheepishly held up his paw and said, "I know that Jesus would love her and be very kind to her. And I know that is what we should do, too. Pastor Penguin, I am very ashamed of the way I've treated Petunia. Tomorrow, I am going to bring a cupcake for her dessert, and I'll eat lunch with her. I also think I need to ask her forgiveness for the way I have treated her."

Pastor Penguin grinned from ear to ear. "Rascal, I can see how sincere you are and how sorry you are for your mistreatment of Petunia. Your attitude now shows how smart you are, and I'm very proud of you."

LIFE APPLICATION PAGE

For Small Group Leaders
• WEEK THREE •

- **Promise Path Action Topic:** Do What Jesus Would Do
- **Desired Outcome:** That kids will focus on doing what Jesus would do by working with an acronym for the word *purity*: P—put away put-downs; U—undo unkind actions; R—run from things you know are wrong; I—invite an adult who loves you to help you; T—think God's thoughts; Y—yell for joy (and high-five) whenever you do what Jesus would do.
- **Bible Story:** Colossians 3:8–9, 12–13
- **Promise Path Memory Verse:** Let us run the race that is before us and never give up. We should remove from our lives anything that would get in the way. And we should remove the sin that so easily catches us. Let us look only to Jesus. Hebrews 12:1–2 (ICB) (older children); We should remove the sin that so easily catches us. Hebrews 12:1 (ICB) (younger children)

THINGS YOU'LL NEED

- Copy of "Tips for Small Group Leaders" (p. 21)
- *Bug Beepers for Promise Keepers* Critter County Activity Book (K–2)
- *Promise Kids on the Promise Path* Children's Journal (3–6)
- Promise Kids Prayer Poster
- Promise Path Action Topic Poster
- Poster board
- Newsprint
- Paper
- Pencils
- Markers
- Chalkboard and chalk

IN ADVANCE

Make a poster for the "PURITY" acronym (above), so that it can be used during your discussion.

KID TALK

The objective of this session is to encourage kids to make choices that will reflect a decision to do what Jesus would do. This is also a good time to reinforce ways kids already follow God's directions. Use these questions to get the group talking.

• **Let's get started today by thinking of some of the things Jesus would do.** (Let kids respond. If they have trouble thinking of some things, make suggestions such as: help others, be kind, show love to others, be friends with someone who has few friends, be honest, say nice things about others, and so on.)

• **Let's think of some of the things we're already doing that Jesus would do.** (Let kids create a list of things they already do that Jesus would do. Celebrate these actions and commend children for following God's directions.)

• **In our story today, the woman in Colosse told us that her church was having trouble doing what Jesus would do. What did the apostle Paul want them to stop doing? What are some of the problems and temptations that you struggle with?** (Let kids identify some of the problems they face. Some may be simple struggles like whether or not to clean their room, while other problems could be on a larger scale. Those problems might include how to forgive a friend who has hurt them or how to say no to an unhealthy habit.)

• **Doing what Jesus would do isn't always easy. But Paul told the people in Colosse that it will bring them God's joy and happiness. Why do think he said that?** (Let kids respond. If necessary, point out that if everyone did what Jesus would do, we would live in a much happier world!)

• **Can you think of anything you need to change to start doing what Jesus would do all day long, every day of the week?** (Let kids respond. Give them some time to think and reflect on their lives and actions. It might take a moment before they are able to answer, and some may not want to answer aloud at all.)

• **Everything Jesus does is considered pure, which means it is genuine, sincere, honest, trustworthy, and pleasing to God. That means everything we do should also be pure. It should come from our heart and be filled with goodness. Our actions should be filled with purity.** (Show kids the "PURITY" poster.) **The word *purity* in this poster is an acronym. Each letter in the word has**

been used to focus on one way we can do what Jesus would do. Let's look at each of these actions and decide how we can put them into practice. (Discuss each of the actions in the acronym. Challenge kids to come up with one way to put away put-downs; undo unkind actions; run from things they know are wrong; invite adults who love them to help; think God's thoughts; and yell for joy and high-five whenever they do what Jesus would do.)
• **Did anyone find a friend to help you follow Jesus last week?** (Let kids share their stories. Celebrate the friendships they talk about.)
• **What did you learn about being friends from your Journal (or Activity Book)?** (Allow kids to respond.) **God wants us to do what Jesus would do. It's the best way we can follow his directions every day of our life!**

GROUP-BUILDING ACTIVITY

(You may want to do this activity earlier in the session.)

If time permits, do the following group-building activity. Ask everyone to stand up. Play this game to help kids get to know what they have in common with others as well as to think about different ways to respond to doing what Jesus would do. Read each of the following items. As each item is read, kids stand on one side of the room to respond to the answer *a* or the other side of the room to respond to the answer *b*. Kids stay in the middle if they are not sure. Ask the children to discuss their answers. There may not be one right way to respond to each case.

1. You promised your little brother you'd play a game with him. Now your best friend wants to go shopping. You: a) go shopping, or b) play the game with your little brother.
2. Your mom isn't feeling well. You: a) make a card to cheer her up, or b) clean up the house so that she doesn't have to.
3. No matter how hard you try, you never get good grades on your math tests. You have another one tomorrow, but today's weather is great! You: a) go out and play—who needs to study? or b) continue to study, trying to get the best grade you can.
4. A new girl just moved into your neighborhood from out of state. You: a) feel more comfortable playing with your own friends, or b) invite her to meet your friends the next time you go to the park.
5. You broke your mom's music box by winding it up too tight after she told you not to. You: a) put it back where it was and hope she doesn't notice, or b) confess you made a mistake and ask her to forgive you.

Continue this game as long as you desire, making up new situations to challenge kids to think about doing what Jesus would do.

PRAYER TALK

Let's begin by praying together our Promise Kids Prayer. At the end of the prayer, we'll ask God to help us to be like Jesus. Then each of us can name one way we'll try to be like Jesus this week.
Using the Promise Kids Prayer Poster, read the prayer together with your group. Encourage kids to finish the prayer, if they feel comfortable, by sharing one way to be like Jesus this week. Be sure to ask the group about any special prayer concerns, requests, or celebrations, and end by praying for each one.

SMALL GROUP TIP

You are now three weeks into the process of getting to know one another. This is a good time to put everyone's name into a paper bag. Then ask each child to draw a name, making sure they do not receive their own. The person whose name they draw will be their prayer pal for the remainder of the Adventure. Ask kids to pray for their partners each week, caring for each other, just like Jesus does.

WEEK FOUR OVERVIEW

- **Promise Path Action Topic:** Make Family Time Important
- **Desired Outcome:** That kids will make family time important by coming up with family ideas, doing simple "family builders" (acts of service) each day, and planning a fun time with their family this week.
- **Bible Story:** Genesis 50:19–21
- **Promise Path Memory Verse:** "Honor your father and mother." This is the first command that has a promise with it. The promise is: "Then everything will be well with you." Ephesians 6:2–3 (ICB) (older children); Honor your father and mother. Ephesians 6:2 (ICB) (younger children)
- **Bible Story Presentation:** Joseph and Reuben will tell the story.
- **Life Application Projects:** The Life Application Projects that correlate with the Promise Path Action Topic for Week 4 are "Promise Path Family Mailbox" (p. 96) and "Promise Path Family Coupons" (p. 89).

Getting Started

As the children arrive, have them check in at the Adventure table, pick up their color-coded name tags, and meet their Small Group leaders. They can then proceed to work on the Life Application Project of their choice or move to the Bible Story Time with their Small Group leaders.

LIFE APPLICATION PROJECTS

Continue to offer ongoing projects, adding new ones as your schedule permits. (You can find more detailed information on pp. 84–104 on how to set up and work with the projects.) Consider any new projects that correlate with this week's lesson as noted in the Overview. These projects will help kids experience activities that encourage them to make family time important.

BIBLE STORY TIME

Gather the children together in a large group. They can sit within their Small Group families.

Weekly Activities

Welcome the children back to the Adventure. Proceed by making any necessary announcements, recognizing birthdays, or taking an offering.

Setting the Scene

Things You'll Need: Promise Path Factory Bible Time Machine with the Week 4 Promise Path Action Topic, Conveyor Belt with this week's Promise Path Memory Verse, a Construction Zone Ahead sign, and construction clothes (bib overalls or jeans, flannel shirt, hard hat). Set up your Factory with a few construction supplies displayed, such as a sawhorse, a ladder, a bucket, paint cans, and so on.

PREPARATION

Dress as a construction worker today (see above). You will also need two people, dressed up as Joseph and his brother Reuben. They will be hidden inside the Bible Time Machine. Provide a copy of the script in the Bible Story Presentation below.

Write this week's Promise Path Action Topic on a piece of paper large enough for kids to read. Then slip the paper into the Factory's Time Machine for use at the appropriate time during the session. Today's Promise Path Road Sign is the Construction Zone Ahead sign. You will need to set up a construction area in the center of the Factory, using the materials listed above.

TOPIC INTRODUCTION

(Enter the factory dressed as a construction worker.)

Hello, everybody! Welcome back to the Promise Path Factory! I hope everyone tried to do what Jesus would do during the week!

(Act confused as you look around at the construction materials you have displayed.) **What in the world are all of these construction materials for? And it looks like our sign for today is a Construction Zone Ahead sign. Well, it sure looks like a construction zone around here, doesn't it? I don't think we were planning on building a new Promise Path Factory. Hmmm. Well, let's start by talking about what a construction worker does.** (Ask kids to explain what a construction worker does.) **Good answers! A construction worker constructs or builds things. In fact, that helps me to understand why all these construction supplies are here. I told our Administrator that we were going to be builders during this week's Adventure. So, naturally, she (or he) tried to help out by giving us some of the tools we might need to build. But we're going to work on building something a little different. Let's go to our Bible Time Machine to get this** week's Promise Path Action Topic so you can see what I mean. (Go to the Time Machine and pull out the topic.) **Let's read it together. "Make Family Time Important." Does anyone have an idea what that has to do with building?** (Let kids respond.) **We're going to be family builders! What sorts of things do you think a family builder might do?** (Let kids respond. Answers might include care for one another, help each other, support each other, spend time together, and so on.)

Family builders make family time important. There are lots of opportunities for kids and grown-ups to get involved in many wonderful things! But getting involved in one thing can often mean taking time away from something else. And no matter how busy we get, God never wants us to ignore our families. He wants us to be family builders who make time for one another because we know it's important!

Today's Bible story is about a man named Joseph. He came from a really big family that had a lot of problems. But no matter how big the family got, or how bad the problems were, Joseph loved his family with all his heart. Let's turn on our Bible Time Machine so we can go back into Bible times to hear someone from Joseph's family tell us what it was like. (Turn on the Bible Time Machine until Joseph and Reuben emerge.)

Bible Story Presentation

Bible Basis: Genesis 50:19–21 (Genesis 37–50 as background)
Storytellers: Joseph and his brother Reuben

Things You'll Need: A Bible-time costume for Joseph and Reuben. Joseph should be wearing a very colorful coat or cape over his tunic.

Today's story is a sketch by Joseph and his brother Reuben. Reuben was Jacob's firstborn son by his wife Leah. Reuben convinced his brothers not to kill Joseph and had intentions of later rescuing him. But his rescue plan failed.

REUBEN: It's great to be here today, all the way from the land of Egypt. My name is Reuben, and this is my brother Joseph.
JOSEPH: Nice to meet all of you!
REUBEN: I'm Joseph's oldest brother, and I want to tell you about him today.
JOSEPH: Be nice, Reuben.
REUBEN: Who, me? I'm always nice.

JOSEPH: (Shields his mouth from Reuben as he whispers loudly to the audience.) Most of the time, anyway.
REUBEN: You may have heard Joseph's story before. There's quite a big story about Joseph and his coat of many colors that our father gave him. You see, Joseph was my father's favorite son because he was born at a time when Father didn't think he would have any more children. Joseph was Father's eleventh son!
JOSEPH: If your mom and dad think it's noisy at your house, well, they should try having twelve sons to deal with all at one time!
REUBEN: We also had a sister. Our family was large, but we worked together to take care of Father's livestock and sheep. We weren't too happy about the fact that Joseph was our father's favorite child. We thought we were all pretty good sons.
JOSEPH: They were good, most of the time, anyway.
REUBEN: Joseph began having dreams about how he was greater than the rest of us and how we would all bow down to him someday.
JOSEPH: I had no control over my dreams, Reuben. They just popped into my head whenever I was asleep!
REUBEN: Well, the rest of us were pretty mad about that. My brothers and I had had it up to here (indicate with hand) with Joseph's dreams. So we thought we would teach him a lesson.
JOSEPH: But God taught them one instead.
REUBEN: That isn't until much later. Anyway, we started to plan and scheme ways to get back at him. Some of my brothers were so angry that they even thought about killing him!
JOSEPH: You never told me that, Reuben!
REUBEN: Oh, well you needn't worry, because I was able to calm them down a bit. Rather than kill Joseph, I suggested that they throw him into a deep hole. Then I planned to secretly return later and rescue him. After all, he was our brother. And even though we were angry, we really did love one another.
JOSEPH: I always knew you loved me, Reuben. But it made me sad when you were mad at me.
REUBEN: The rest of our brothers agreed. They started by taking away Joseph's beautiful coat. Then they threw him in the deep hole.
JOSEPH: It was awful in there!
REUBEN At least it wasn't filled with water.
JOSEPH: No, but it was dark, cold, and hard to breathe in there. And whew, was it stinky!
REUBEN: After I was sure Joseph was safe in the pit, I went out to tend Father's sheep, so I wasn't around for what happened next. Some travelers came by, and my brothers decided to sell Joseph to them as a slave.
JOSEPH: So much for getting rescued!
REUBEN: Years went by. And none of us ever gave

much more thought to poor Joseph. But Joseph led quite an exciting life. He was sold again . . .
JOSEPH: Which was good.
REUBEN: Traded . . .
JOSEPH: Which was okay . . .
REUBEN: And imprisoned . . .
JOSEPH: Which was definitely not my idea of fun.
REUBEN: But he was eventually put in charge of the land of Egypt.
JOSEPH: Now that was pretty cool.
REUBEN: You see, his dreams and their interpretations turned out to be quite important. They were so important that he was able to interpret one of Pharaoh's dreams.
JOSEPH: Pharaoh was the king of Egypt. He had a dream that was really bothering him. But, with God's help, I was able to tell him what his dream meant. The dream said that the king would have seven wonderful years of great harvest. This made the king very happy. His dream also said that those years would be followed by seven years of famine (that means no food). That worried the king, but he was pleased to know about it well ahead of time.
REUBEN: Pharaoh was so impressed that he made Joseph his second in command. As you probably guessed, everything Joseph said came true.
JOSEPH: Yep! There were seven years of great harvest. And then a time of great famine. But God helped me plan wisely for that time, and all the people of Egypt still had plenty to eat.
REUBEN: My family, however, did not know about the upcoming famine, so Father sent us to the land of Egypt where they had so wisely stored their food and grain. We begged Pharaoh's second in command for food so that we would not starve. We didn't know were were talking to Joseph!
JOSEPH: They came and bowed down before me, just like I had dreamed about many years before. But the best part was that they didn't recognize me as their brother. What do you think I did? (*Let the kids respond.*)
REUBEN: Joseph is an amazing man. He followed God's direction and did what was pleasing to God. Joseph knew that his family was important.
JOSEPH: That's why I forgave them, because I still loved them very much.
REUBEN: You can imagine how scared we were! But Joseph hugged us, and asked us to get our father so we could all live together in Egypt. And we did. Because a family needs to be together.
JOSEPH: You see, even though my brothers had planned to hurt me, it had been God's plan all along, not theirs. And because of God's plan, I was able to save many lives—even my brothers' lives—during the years of famine.

REUBEN: Joseph promised to provide for us and our children, and always spoke kindly to us. Because Joseph knew the importance of family. Thank you, Joseph.
JOSEPH: You're welcome, Reuben. But I was just doing what God wanted me to do . . .
REUBEN: To care for our families and make time for each other in our busy lives.
JOSEPH: (*to children*) I hope you'll make family time important, too.

Comprehension Questions
Briefly discuss these questions with the children to clarify the main ideas in the Bible Story Presentation.
• **Why were Joseph's brothers so angry and jealous of him?** (Because he was treated as the favorite son. He also had dreams that said the others would have to bow down to him, as if he were better than them.)
• **What did Joseph's brothers do to him?** (They threw him in a deep hole, then sold him as a slave.)
• **How did this turn into something good for Joseph and others?** (Pharaoh had a dream that Joseph was able to explain. The dream said that there would be seven years of great harvest followed by seven years of famine. Pharaoh was so impressed that he made Joseph his second in command. That way Joseph was able to plan wisely for the years of famine and saved many lives.)
• **What happened when Joseph's brothers came to him asking for food?** (Joseph forgave them. Then he invited his brothers and father to come live with him in Egypt.)
• **Why was Joseph kind to his brothers?** (Because he followed God's directions and knew that families were important.)

Promise Path Memory Verse
Things You'll Need: Week 4's Promise Path Memory Verse (Ephesians 6:2–3) written on the scroll inside the Conveyor Belt. You will also need some wooden blocks with today's memory verse written on them for each Small Group (see below). You can use masking tape if you don't want to write directly on the blocks. If you don't have blocks available, substitute another building material such as cups or plastic containers.

I need a volunteer to help me crank up our Conveyor Belt to discover today's Promise Path Memory Verse. (Choose a volunteer and crank the lever of your Conveyor Belt until today's verse is showing.)

Let's read what it says. "Honor your father and mother." This is the first command that has a promise with it. The promise is: "Then everything will be well with you." How can we honor our father and mother? (Let kids respond. Answers might include love them, respect them, trust them, be kind and helpful to them, and so on.) **Why will everything be well with us if we do that?** (Because God has given us parents to take care of us. If we honor them, then we will be following God's direction and making our family important.)

Let's play a memory verse game today. I have a group of blocks for each Small Group. Each block has one word (or phrase) of today's memory verse written on it. Your job is to put the memory verse in order, while trying to build the highest tower you can. Ready? Begin! (Let kids assemble the blocks in order, while trying to build a tower. Compare towers when everyone's finished.)

Younger children can learn a shortened version of the verse—"Honor your father and mother." Ephesians 6:2—if you choose to split the group in half. Say the words, one at a time. The kids can find each word as it is said and put the block in the appropriate place.

LIFE APPLICATION SMALL GROUP TIME

Dismiss the children with their Small Group leaders, taking care to let the groups farthest away from the meeting area leave first. Each Small Group leader will need a copy of the Life Application page for today (p. 55). Be sure to give the page to leaders at least a week ahead of time so that they can be ready to work with their groups.

CHILDREN'S CHURCH WORSHIP

Things You'll Need: *Promise Kids Sing-along* cassette, audiocasette player, and an offering basket.

If you are using this section, be sure to allow kids a short time to stand up and stretch in between activities. You might also want to include some active songs during the singing time.

Singing

Choose music that fits the theme of this week's Promise Path Action Topic: Make Family Time Important. To reinforce this week's Promise Path Memory Verse, teach the song "Honor Your Father and Your Mother" on page 114 of this leader's guide. The song can be found on the *Promise Kids Sing-along*

audiocassette. (See p. 128 for ordering information.)

Critter County Story

Through the familiar and friendly Critter County characters, the children can see this week's theme in action and be motivated to follow God's directions by making family time important. This week's story begins on page 54.

Offering

One way children can learn to worship and respond to God is by giving. If you are using this curriculum for a children's church program, you may prefer to take the offering now instead of during the Weekly Activities portion of the Bible Story Time. Encourage children to think about their family as they thank God for something, either verbally or silently, when they pass the offering basket.

Praise and Prayer

Continue to help children through a prayer experience by offering them a line and asking them to repeat it. (Refer to Week 1, p. 32.) This week, encourage children to think about one way to make family time important during the week. Let the children conclude the prayer time with their own sentences, asking God to help them follow his directions.

MIDWEEK EXTRAS

Things You'll Need: *Promise Kids Sing-along* cassette and audiocassette player.

Game
FAMILIES ARE IMPORTANT!
Have kids walk around the room, greeting one another or singing as the music plays. (You can use this week's song, "Honor Your Father and Your Mother," or other songs on the cassette.) When the music stops, divide kids into small family groups of a specific number. For example, say: "Create family groups of three!" (When there are an odd number of children, simply add one or two to another group.) Groups of three then gather together and must share one idea with each other of how to make family time important. Continue by playing the music again. When the music stops, kids must try to get into a new family group. Again, share ideas with new family members. Continue play as long as desired.

 ADJUSTMENT FOR YOUNGER AGES
Suggest that older children and younger

children find family groups together. Older children can help younger ones come up with ideas by prompting them with questions like, "What is something you can do that would help your mom and dad at home?" or "What's something fun you like to do with your family?"

If you have only younger children in your group, the leader can ask the prompting questions.

Singing

Singing is a fun way to praise God. Make use of the songs included in this book, beginning on page 105. Be sure to learn the song "Honor Your Father and Your Mother" on page 114 of this leader's guide. The song can be found on the *Promise Kids Sing-along* cassette. And remember to include some active songs to give kids an opportunity to move around.

Critter County Story
THE BEST OF BOTH WORLDS

"I got 'em, I got 'em! Hey, Lunchbox, I got the tickets to the ball game this Saturday," shouted Lester the lion as he came in the front door. "Oh, Lunchbox, oh, joy of my life. Did you hear me? I got the tickets!"

Liona Lou and Lunchbox came in the back door of the lion's den. "Oh, Lester, you're *home!*" shrieked Liona Lou as she ran over to give her husband a big welcome-home hug.

"Dad, what were you saying about tickets?" asked Lunchbox.

With a smirk and a wave of his strong arm, Lester announced once again, "I got the tickets to the big game on Saturday. They aren't great seats, but we'll be there, my boy!"

"Hold onto your travel horse, Lester. Did you forget? This Saturday is the family reunion. *Everyone* from my side of the family will be there and most of your relatives as well," said Liona Lou.

Well, the king of the jungle slumped against the wall of the lion's den and s-l-o-w-l-y sank to the floor. "Oh, my life is over. Oh, woe is me. We have tickets to the big game and I'm going to be eating burned beans with a bunch of lions whose names I don't even know."

"Oh, Lester," said Liona Lou as she tried to comfort her sad husband. You know their names. There's Auntie Penelope Pistachio from Pittsburgh and Uncle Horatio Geraldo from Toledo."

"Mom, can't we skip the reunion this year and pick it up next time?" asked little Lunchbox.

"I know you would both enjoy the game, but we have made a commitment to our family to attend the reunion. And besides, everyone will be looking for-

ward to the dish I'm bringing. I plan to serve my specialty, eggplant eclairs and tossed, toasted toadstools."

No one mentioned the ball game the rest of the week. Lester and Lunchbox were too sad at the thought that they were going to miss the big game. Finally, Saturday morning arrived and everyone got up early to get ready for the family reunion. Lester and Lunchbox were trying hard to make the best of the situation, but their hearts were going to the ball park while their bodies were headed toward the picnic. "I just can't believe we have to miss the game, Dad," said Lunchbox as they were loading the car.

Just as they were ready to lock the front door, Lester heard the phone ringing inside. "Hold on, I'm coming," he said as he crossed the living room to the phone. "Hellllllo!"

"Hey, Lester. This is your ol' Cousin Clementine. How are you, boy?" roared the lion on the other end.

"Oh, we're just purring on all four paws. Are you coming to the reunion, Clementine?"

"Well, normally I wouldn't miss it for the world. Aunt Matilda's mushroom and mayonnaise meatloaf is to growl for, but I have something to offer you and Lunchbox. I got a whole block of tickets given to me for the big game this afternoon, right down front. All the sports fans want to go and celebrate our family by having a game day out. The others want to relax at the picnic and catch up on everyone's news. You and that boy of yours want to go?"

Lester could hardly believe his ears, and he almost jumped through the phone. "Do we want to go? *Do we want to go?*" shouted Lester.

And with that booming voice attracting all the attention, Liona Lou and Lunchbox came bounding in through the front door. "What's going on?" asked Liona.

Well, Lunchbox about jumped up and hit the ceiling when he heard the news. "You mean we can be with our family *and* go to the game? This is going to be the best day of our life!"

Liona Lou put her head on Lester's shoulder as he drove to the picnic. "I'm so glad you get to go to the game, Lester. And I want to thank you for putting our family first and agreeing to come to the picnic even when it looked like you would miss the game."

"Oh, Liona Lou," said Lester with a grin on his lips. "As much as I love to go to the games, the idea of being together and enjoying homemade apple pie with you by my side and Lunchbox at my paws is better than winning the World Series."

LIFE APPLICATION PAGE

For Small Group Leaders
• WEEK FOUR •

- **Promise Path Action Topic:** Make Family Time Important
- **Desired Outcome:** That kids will make family time important by coming up with family ideas, doing simple "family builders" (acts of service) each day, and planning a fun time with their family this week.
- **Bible Story:** Genesis 50:19–21
- **Promise Path Memory Verse:** "Honor your father and mother." This is the first command that has a promise with it. The promise is: "Then everything will be well with you." Ephesians 6:2–3 (ICB) (older children); Honor your father and mother. Ephesians 6:2 (ICB) (younger children)

THINGS YOU'LL NEED

- Copy of "Tips for Small Group Leaders" (p. 21)
- *Bug Beepers for Promise Keepers* Critter County Activity Book (K–2)
- *Promise Kids on the Promise Path* Children's Journal (3–6)
- Promise Kids Prayer Poster
- Promise Path Action Topic Poster
- Newsprint
- Markers
- Chalkboard and chalk
- Soft, spongy ball

KID TALK

This week's Promise Path Action Topic focuses on making family time important. Begin with a brainstorming session listing all of the good things that can happen when families work together. Then make a separate list of all the potential things that can happen when families don't work together. Use these questions to further your discussion:
• **Why do you think people let themselves get super busy?** (Allow the children to voice their opinions. Explain that getting involved to help others by contributing time to school, clubs, sports, and church is good! But making so many commitments to others can sometimes mean ignoring our own family, and that's bad. God wants us to help others but not at the expense of hurting our family.)
• **Why are families so important?** (Answers might include anything from being the people we can always trust and count on to being where we're loved as ourselves.)
• **What did Joseph do to show the importance of family?** (He forgave his family, helped them when they were hungry, and then offered them a new place to live where he would help to care for them.)

• **What are ways you can make family time more important?** (Allow kids to respond.)
• **What's a fun activity you could suggest for your family to do together?** (Allow kids to respond.)
• **What is one simple way you could serve your family this week?** (Some ideas are: volunteer for a chore that you don't usually do, thank your mom or dad for what they do, encourage someone who is feeling sad, and so on.)
• **How many of you practiced doing what Jesus would do last week?** (Let kids share their answers and stories. Celebrate their efforts.)
• **What did you learn from your Journal (or Activity Book) about doing what Jesus would do?** (Allow kids to respond.) **We only get one family. It's important to take care of one another, love one another, and make our time together special.**

GROUP-BUILDING ACTIVITY
(You may want to do this activity earlier in the session.)

If time permits, do the following group-building activity. Ask everyone to sit in a circle. Have kids toss the ball into each other's laps haphazardly across the circle. Each time children catch the ball, they should share something about themselves and say one way they will try to make family time important this week. Continue until everyone has had at least one turn.

PRAYER TALK

Today during our prayer time, we want to think about how we can make our family time important. Let's begin by reading our Promise Path Prayer and then ask God to help us as we name one way to make family time important this week.

Using the Promise Path Prayer Poster, read the prayer together with your group. Encourage kids to finish the prayer by promising one way to make family time more important this week. Be sure to ask the group about any special prayer concerns, requests, or celebrations, and end by praying for each one.

SMALL GROUP TIP

As your group gets to know one another better, you will not only observe developing friendships, but you may also notice that several children are having trouble fitting in. (If that's not the case, then celebrate the positive relationships being built in your group.) Be very sensitive to this. It's easy to focus on the joy of growing and learning how to be Promise Kids. Take an inventory of what is being shared in your group. Has everyone had a chance to share his or her ideas and answers?

Because some students will be particularly cautious about opening up to others, you don't need to require everyone's participation in any given discussion. But you do want to look for opportunities for timid students and allow them time to expand on their answers by asking one or two follow-up questions as well. And let everyone know that their honest answers are appreciated and respected.

WEEK FIVE OVERVIEW

- **Promise Path Action Topic:** Get Involved at Church
- **Desired Outcome:** That kids will become God's family builders at church by getting involved and by choosing one way to encourage another child or adult at church.
- **Bible Story:** Acts 4:32–37; 9:26–28; 13:1–15:35
- **Promise Path Memory Verse:** You should not stay away from church meetings, as some are doing. But you should meet together and encourage each other. Hebrews 10:25 (ICB) (older children); You should meet together and encourage each other. Hebrews 10:25 (ICB) (younger children)
- **Bible Story Presentation:** A news reporter will interview Barnabas.
- **Life Application Projects:** The Life Application Projects that correlate with the Promise Path Action Topic for Week 5 are "Promise Path Church Calendar" (p. 89), "Make a Difference Gift Cards" (p. 103), and "Promise Packages" (p. 91).

Getting Started

As the children arrive, have them check in at the Adventure table, pick up their color-coded name tags, and meet their Small Group leaders. They can then proceed to work on the Life Application Project of their choice or move to the Bible Story Time with their Small Group leaders.

LIFE APPLICATION PROJECTS

Continue to offer ongoing projects, adding new ones as your schedule permits. (You can find more detailed information on pp. 84–104 on how to set up and work with the projects.) Consider any new projects that correlate with this week's lesson as noted in the Overview. Those projects will help kids experience activities that encourage them to get involved at church.

BIBLE STORY TIME

Gather the children together in a large group. They can sit within their Small Group families.

Weekly Activities

Welcome the children back to the Adventure. Proceed by making any necessary announcements, recognizing birthdays, or taking an offering.

Setting the Scene

Things You'll Need: Promise Path Factory Bible Time Machine with this week's Promise Path Action Topic, Conveyor Belt with this week's Promise Path Memory Verse, a Merge sign, and factory clothes.

PREPARATION

Dress as a factory worker today. You will also need someone dressed up in Bible-time clothes as Barnabas and a modern-day news reporter. They will be hidden inside the Bible Time Machine. Provide a copy of the script in the Bible Story Presentation below.

Write the Promise Path Action Topic for Week 5 on a piece of paper large enough for kids to read. Then slip the week's topic into the Factory's Time Machine for use at the appropriate time during the session. Today's Promise Path Road Sign is the Merge sign.

TOPIC INTRODUCTION

(Enter the Factory dressed as a factory worker.)

Hello! Are you ready to get back on the Promise Path and learn how to follow God's directions? I hope so! Last week we learned how to make family time important. I need a volunteer to come and help me get this week's Promise Path Action Topic out of our Bible Time Machine. (Allow a volunteer to pull this week's topic out of the machine.) Let's read it together. "Get involved at church." How many of you already get involved at church? (Let the kids respond.) All of you should have raised your hand, because all of you are here at church today. That means you're already on your way to following God's direction about church!

Today's sign is the Merge sign. (Show your sign to the children.) What does the word *merge* mean? (Let kids respond.) Merging means to blend, to mix, to join, or to get involved with something, and today's something is getting involved at church. Let's try a merge experiment. Let's begin by standing up. (Encourage all of the children to stand.)

Every time I hold up the Merge sign, I'll call out a command. Your job will be to merge with other people around you while following the

command. Ready? Let's begin. (Hold up your sign, then give the following commands:)
- Shake your neighbor's hand.
- Give your neighbor a high-five.
- Rub your neighbor's back.
- Find out your neighbor's favorite color.
- Find out your neighbor's favorite food.

Great job merging! You were so good that I don't think you'll have any trouble merging with this week's Promise Path Action Topic, get involved at church! After merging with one another this morning, can anyone think of ways we can merge in our church? (Let kids respond.) There are many ways we can get more involved at church, and you're on the right path toward getting there.

Let's go to our Bible Time Machine so we can talk to a man named Barnabas. Barnabas was involved in a lot of merging back in Bible times. Let's find out how. (Turn on the Time Machine until Barnabas appears.)

Bible Story Presentation
Bible Basis: Acts 4:32–37; 9:26–28; 13:1–15:35
Storytellers: Barnabas and Curious Kate (or Cal), a news reporter

Things You'll Need: A Bible-time costume for Barnabas, and two comfy chairs set up next to and slightly turned toward one another as on a late-night interview show.

Today's story is an interview with one of the first missionaries of the church, Barnabas. He was regarded as an apostle and was probably one of the 72 followers of Christ (Luke 10:1).

(Curious Kate and Barnabas sit in chairs across from one another. Barnabas takes the chair to the right of his interviewer.)

CURIOUS: Welcome to the Stay-up-Late-with-Curious-Kate Show! My name is Curious Kate, and I'm called Curious because there's always something more I want to know. My guest for tonight is a man named Barnabas who comes—originally—from the city of Jerusalem. Hello, Barnabas, welcome to the show!
BARNABAS: Hello, Curious. It's good to be here!
CURIOUS: First, I'm curious about your funny name. What does Barnabas mean?
BARNABAS: Well, actually, Curious, my real name is Joseph. But people call me Barnabas because I love to help, and Barnabas means "Son of Encouragement."

CURIOUS: Well, that's curious. Who is it that you love to help?
BARNABAS: Mostly I love to help my church. You see, church is very important to me, so I do whatever I can to get involved.
CURIOUS: How very curious! Is this a usual condition among church people?
BARNABAS: Back in Bible times when the church first started, it was indeed usual! In fact, nearly *everyone* wanted to get involved with the church—people were so happy to be together all the time that it looked like we all lived together!
CURIOUS: My, my! And just to satisfy my curiosity, can you tell me whether this is still the case in churches?
BARNABAS: Hmm. That's a good question. Perhaps we should ask our studio audience.
CURIOUS: Great idea! *(to children)* How about it, all you viewers out there? Do you love to help your church? *(Allow kids to respond.)* And what about the other people you know? Do most others also love to help the church? *(Answers may vary.)*
BARNABAS: You know, Curious, many people get involved in *ministries* in their church.
CURIOUS: Wait, hold it—my curiosity is getting the best of me. What's a ministry?
BARNABAS: A ministry is a way of pulling people in the church together and helping one another out. It involves a whole lifestyle of getting involved—my favorite subject!
CURIOUS: But isn't ministry what a minister or pastor does?
BARNABAS: No, no! *Everyone* in the church can do some kind of ministry! Helping our pastor to help the church is something we all need to be doing as much as we can.
CURIOUS: For curiosity's sake, let me ask: Were you involved in ministries back in your day? And what was that like?
BARNABAS: Oh, yes, I was very involved with the church. I really enjoyed giving to people who didn't have as much as I did—that was one of my ministries. You know, God kindly provided some land for me, and I sold the land and gave the money to the church. That way I could be kind to the poor people!
CURIOUS: So you gave money to the poor and then were considered a "son of encouragement"?
BARNABAS: Actually, Curious, that's not all there is to it. Being a "son of encouragement" is more than a one-time deal. Let me tell you, I love the church so much, I just want to help its people out all the time! And that's why I was part of a welcoming ministry.
CURIOUS: My curiosity is killing me. I've got to know: What is a welcoming ministry?

BARNABAS: May I suggest that we get someone from our studio audience to help me demonstrate? *(to children)* Who would like to volunteer? *(Pick someone to stand front and center and play "Saul.")* I had the opportunity to welcome one of my best friends, Paul, to the church. Did I hear correctly, studio audience, that you met my friend Paul a couple of weeks ago? *(Allow for response.)* Well, Paul (whose name was *Saul* when I first met him) had been a terrible enemy of my church. One day he showed up and said he was a Christian *(Have the child point to the sky and say, "I saw the Lord Jesus Christ!")*—and no one believed him! So he was feeling a little left out. I wanted to do everything I could to welcome him to our church. So I brought him to other people in the church. *(Put your arm around "Saul's" shoulder and step forward as if to speak to the audience as the "church.")* And I introduced him around. *(Introduce "Saul" to several of the kids and help them shake hands.)* I just started including him in every church gathering, and pretty soon he was good friends with us all! *(Give the kid a high-five and sit down.)* That's what ministry looks like, Curious.

CURIOUS: That's fascinating! You mentioned you were involved in several kinds of ministry. What else did you do, Barnabas?

BARNABAS: Oh, let's see. I was honored to be one of the first missionaries sent out from Antioch, the city in Syria where I had been teaching. I also served as a messenger several times—doesn't seem like an important job, but I was just happy to be helping out.

CURIOUS: So you're saying we can be involved in the church by teaching, giving our money to church, and telling others about Jesus and inviting them to church?

BARNABAS: Yes, but our studio audience might be interested to know that we can also be involved by doing more simple things—like running errands for other people who are helping the church, or welcoming and including new people or those who feel left out. And most importantly, we can get involved in church just by coming whenever we can!

CURIOUS: You know, our floor director is giving me the cue that our show time's almost up. Thank you for visiting with us on the Stay-Up-Late-with-Curious-Kate Show, Barnabas. You've been very helpful and encouraging to us all.

BARNABAS: My pleasure, Curious Kate. But just one more thing—

CURIOUS: What's that?

BARNABAS: Now *I'm* curious. *(Turn to the children.)* How are you going to get involved at church?

Comprehension Questions

Briefly discuss these questions with the children to clarify the main ideas in the Bible story presentation.

• **What does the name *Barnabas* mean, and why did it describe him so well?** (It means "Son of Encouragement," which describes his wanting to help people in the church as much as possible.)

• **What is *ministry?*** (Ministry is a lifestyle of getting involved. It's a way of pulling people in the church together and helping one another out.)

• **What are some kinds of ministries, or ways of getting involved?** (Some ministries are: telling others about Jesus and bringing them to church, welcoming newcomers, including those who might feel left out, teaching, giving money, running errands or helping people who are doing work for the church.)

• **What's the most important way we can get involved at church?** (We can best get involved by coming to church as much as we can.)

Promise Path Memory Verse

Things You'll Need: Promise Path Memory Verse (Hebrews 10:25) written on a the scroll inside the Conveyor Belt.

I need a volunteer to help me crank up our Conveyor Belt to discover our Promise Path Memory Verse. (Choose a volunteer and crank the lever of your Conveyor Belt until today's verse is showing.)

Let's read what it says. **"You should not stay away from the church meetings, as some are doing. But you should meet together and encourage each other."** That's just what Barnabas told us, isn't it? He encouraged us to get involved at church, worship regularly, and go to other church activities and meetings so that we can encourage each other to love Jesus and do good deeds.

Let's get involved at church today by working together to learn our memory verse. How many of you have heard of "the wave"? (Allow children to respond and briefly describe it.) **The wave is often done at school or sporting events to get the crowd involved in whatever is going on. I'm going to separate our crowd into six groups. Then I'm going to assign each group one part of today's verse. As you say your part of the verse, your group needs to stand up and wave their arms in the air until you are done with your part of the verse. Then sit down while the next group takes over.**

Assign six groups the following parts of the verse. This activity will work with a small or large group.

1) You should not stay away;
2) from the church meetings;
3) as some are doing.
4) But you should meet together;
5) and encourage each other.
6) Hebrews 10:25

Repeat the activity until the entire group knows the verse well, speeding up after you get really good. If you have an advanced group, try it again, but assign the verse parts in reverse.

 If you choose to split the group in half, younger children can learn a shortened version of the verse—"You should meet together and encourage each other." Hebrews 10:25.

LIFE APPLICATION SMALL GROUP TIME

Dismiss the children with their Small Group leaders, taking care to let the groups farthest away from the meeting area leave first. Each Small Group leader will need a copy of the Life Application page for today (p. 62). Be sure to give the page to leaders at least a week ahead of time so that they can be ready to work with their groups.

CHILDREN'S CHURCH WORSHIP

Things You'll Need: *Promise Kids Sing-along* cassette, audiocasette player, and an offering basket.

If you are using this section, be sure to allow kids a short time to stand up and stretch in between activities. You might also want to include some active songs during the singing time.

Singing
Choose music that fits the theme of this week's Promise Path Action Topic: Get Involved at Church. To reinforce this week's Promise Path Memory Verse, teach the song "You Should Meet Together" on page 116 of this leader's guide. The song can be found on the *Promise Kids Sing-along* cassette. (See p. 128 for ordering information.)

Critter County Story
Through the familiar and friendly Critter County characters, the children can see this week's theme in action and be motivated to follow God's directions by getting involved at church. This week's story begins on page 61.

Offering
One way children can learn to worship and respond to God is by giving. If you are using this curriculum for a children's church program, you may prefer to take the offering now instead of during the Weekly Activities portion of the Bible Story Time. Encourage children to think about their church as they thank God for something, either verbally or silently, when they pass the offering basket.

Praise and Prayer
Continue to help children through a prayer experience by offering them a line and asking them to repeat it. (Refer to Week 1, p. 32.) Encourage children to think about one way to get involved at church this week. Let the children conclude the prayer time with their own sentences, asking God to help them follow his directions.

MIDWEEK EXTRAS

Things You'll Need: *Promise Kids Sing-along* cassette, audiocassette player, two shoe boxes, paper (two pieces per child), pencils, and a large box or laundry basket. In the basket put items such as a get well card, a bag of flour, a Bible, a measuring cup, a wallet, a doll, a canned good, a toy, and so on.

Game
GET INVOLVED AT CHURCH!
Give two pieces of paper and pencil to each child. Tell them to write down the title of a person on one piece of paper (such as mom, grandpa, nurse, lawyer, minister), and a place (such as home, school, hospital, park, store) on another sheet of paper.

Collect the papers and place them in the box or basket with the items above. Each child will get a turn to select a person out of one box, a place out of the other, and one item out of the basket. That child must then come up with one way that *person* can do something at that *place* with that *item* for their church. For example, a *mom* can buy some *flour* at the *store* to make cookies for her child's Sunday school class; or a *doctor* can invite his or her son's teacher at the *school* to worship with a *Bible* on Sunday. Some of the ideas will undoubtedly take some imagination, but it will be a fun way to get kids thinking of creative ways to get involved at church.

 ADJUSTMENT FOR YOUNGER AGES
Suggest that older children and younger children work together in selecting and coming

up with ways to get involved at church. Or just put out the basket of items and see if kids can think of ways they relate to the church. For example: a baby rattle is used by people who work in the church nursery, a choir folder is used by people who sing in the church choir, and so on.

Singing

Singing is a fun way to praise God. Make use of the songs included in this book, beginning on page 105. Be sure to learn the song "You Should Meet Together" on page 116 of this leader's guide. The song can be found on the *Promise Kids Sing-along* cassette. And remember to include some active songs to give kids an opportunity to move around.

Critter County Story

HIP, HIP HOORAY! IT'S SUNDAY SCHOOL DAY
"I wish Grandmother Mouse would come back from her long trip. I miss her so much as our Sunday school teacher," said Petunia the sweet-smelling little skunk.

"Yeah, Mr. Moose is trying hard, but he has never taught before," answered Rascal the raccoon. "And his antlers get in the way when he tries to write on the chalkboard. Everybody just sits there. We don't sing and we never answer his questions."

"Hey, Rascal," said Petunia, "maybe we would all have more fun and learn more if we helped Mr. Moose be a better teacher."

"How do we do that? Saw off his antlers?" asked Rascal.

"No, silly raccoon. We could all help him this Sunday morning. Here's the plan. . ." Petunia told Rascal her idea and they called all the kids in their class and told them the plan.

The following Sunday morning, all the kids were excited to go to Sunday school again. They went to their classroom and could hardly wait for Mr. Moose to get there. Finally, he came just in time to start the music. He walked to the front of the room and seemed discouraged.

"Okay, boys and girls, now it's time to sing," he said very slowly. Much to his surprise, all the critters stood on their feet and paws and had big smiles on their faces. As they began to sing, Mr. Moose's eyes got big. He couldn't believe his ears! All of the critters were singing loud and clear, and their voices blended together like ice cream and syrup. It sound-ed like a choir. Mr. Moose smiled from ear to ear. And that's a big smile on a moose's face!

Next, he began to tell the story. Usually the kids turned around and talked to each other during the lesson. The little owl usually went to sleep and the seal who sat in the back usually played with a ball on his nose.

But not this Sunday. Everyone sat straight in their chairs and listened with both ears. Mr. Moose was delighted as he taught the lesson. The more he talked, the more excited he got, and the more excited he got, the better the story! It was easy for the boys and girls to listen now because the lesson was so interesting.

In fact, Mr. Moose got some chalk and started to draw on the chalkboard. He had never done this before, and his picture was so good, the critters all clapped when he was finished. "It's a masterpiece!" said Rascal.

After the lesson was over, the boys and girls went to the back of the room for craft time. Mr. Moose talked to them about the things they could make that special Sunday morning in Critter County. After he explained everything to the boys and girls, he left the room for a few minutes. While he was gone, Petunia whispered to the others, "Hey, let's make a picture for Mr. Moose. Lunchbox, you can draw the best. Would you get us started?"

So Lunchbox started the picture, and everyone helped. They had just finished when Mr. Moose walked back into the room. Rascal said, "Mr. Moose, would you please close your eyes?" Mr. Moose agreed. Rascal walked up to the front of the room and handed the rolled up picture to the teacher.

With much surprise and delight on his face, the very happy teacher opened his gift. He saw the picture of himself teaching the class of critters that Lunchbox had drawn. On his chest was a sign that read, "World's Best Teacher."

A tear of happiness began to roll down the long nose of the moose. "Why, boys and girls, I don't know what to say. No one has ever done anything like this for me before. I feel so honored."

All the kids clapped and cheered as they got their things together to leave. Petunia said what everyone else was thinking. "This was one of the best Sunday school classes we have ever had!" The birds chirped, the owl hooted, and the ducks all quacked because they agreed.

LIFE APPLICATION PAGE

For Small Group Leaders

• WEEK FIVE •

- **Promise Path Action Topic:** Get Involved at Church
- **Desired Outcome:** That kids will become God's family builders at church by getting involved and by choosing one way to encourage another child or adult at church.
- **Bible Story:** Acts 4:32–37; 9:26–28; 13:1–15:35
- **Promise Path Memory Verse:** You should not stay away from church meetings, as some are doing. But you should meet together and encourage each other. Hebrews 10:25 (ICB) (older children); You should meet together and encourage each other. Hebrews 10:25 (ICB) (younger children)

THINGS YOU'LL NEED

- Copy of "Tips for Small Group Leaders" (p. 21)
- *Bug Beepers for Promise Keepers* Critter County Activity Book (K–2)
- *Promise Kids on the Promise Path* Children's Journal (3–6)
- Promise Kids Prayer Poster
- Promise Path Action Topic Poster
- Newsprint
- Markers
- Chalkboard and chalk

KID TALK

This week's Promise Path Action Topic focuses on getting involved at church. Younger children may have more difficulty grasping this idea. If this is the case, concentrate on encouraging kids to ask questions when they don't understand something. You may have to give kids a little background on some of the opportunities your church already offers as ways for children to get involved. (Some kid examples are choir, club, Sunday school, cleanup day, and so on.) Explain what happens at a church education meeting or a church evangelism meeting. Let kids know about any upcoming events like ice cream socials, vacation Bible school, or potluck dinners. Use these questions to further your discussion:

• **Why do you come to church?** (Answers may range from "because Mom and Dad make me" to "I want to learn about God." Accept and affirm all answers. This is a time for kids to explore different opportunities at church.)

• **Why do you think it's important to get involved at church?** (Answers might include encouraging others, to learn more about God, to help others, to have fun, to worship God.)

• **What are some of the ways you can get more involved at church?** (Answers can include ways children, adults, or families can be more involved at church. Encourage kids to think of different ways to get involved, including worship, fun and fellowship, outreach, and service projects that strengthen the church or broader community.)

• **What are some ideas for people to get involved that our church might want to offer in the future?** (Encourage kids to be creative. They may come up with some great future ideas for your education planners!)

• **What are some ways you could encourage someone from church this week?** (Visit a sick or shut-in member, send a note to the pastor or other leaders thanking them for what they do, or make a "Jesus Loves You" poster or banner to hang in the church lobby or hallway.)

• **Did anyone remember to make family time important last week? How?** (Let kids share their stories of special family times during the week. Celebrate their participation and answers.)

• **What did you learn in your Journal (Activity Book) about making family time important?**

GROUP-BUILDING ACTIVITY

(You may want to do this activity earlier in the session.)

If time permits, do the following group-building activity. Have everyone sit in a circle. Choose one person to be "it." "It" will go around to each person and try to make him or her smile by saying, "I'm going to get you involved at church by making you laugh!" The child must respond, "I want to get involved at church, but you can't make me laugh" without smiling. "It" can try to make the person laugh any way possible, without touching. If someone cracks a smile, then that person is the next one to make others laugh.

PRAYER TALK

Today during our prayer time, let's think about how we plan to get involved at church. We can start by asking our parents to help us. Right now, we can ask God to help us. We can thank God for all the things he has given us, and tell him how much we want to spend our time in his presence. Let's begin by reading our Promise Kids Prayer and then ask God to help us as we name one way we'd like to encourage someone from church this week.

Using the Promise Kids Prayer Poster, read the prayer together with your group. Encourage kids to finish the prayer, if they feel comfortable, by choosing one way to encourage someone at church. Be sure to ask the group about any special prayer concerns, requests, or celebrations, and end by praying for each one.

SMALL GROUP TIP

Children are often nervous about praying aloud in front of others. Be sure to let kids know that while God likes it when we pray aloud in a group, he especially likes to hear from us in private. Tell kids that it's a good idea to pray about our very personal thoughts, hopes, problems, and dreams when we are alone. Never pressure a child into praying out loud when he or she feels uncomfortable. Just let children know that God is there for them whenever they need him and will listen whenever they wish to pray.

WEEK SIX OVERVIEW

- **Promise Path Action Topic:** Accept Others as Jesus Does
- **Desired Outcome:** That kids will make an effort to accept others, especially kids their own age. That they will also make a decision to put away put-downs toward others.
- **Bible Story:** Mark 1:40–42
- **Promise Path Memory Verse:** God does not see the same way people see. People look at the outside of a person, but the Lord looks at the heart. 1 Samuel 16:7 (ICB) (older children); People look at the outside of a person, but the Lord looks at the heart. 1 Samuel 16:7 (ICB) (younger children)
- **Bible Story Presentation:** A healed leper will tell the story.
- **Life Application Projects:** The Life Application Projects that correlate with the Promise Path Action Topic for Week 6 are "Promise Path Research" (p. 94) and "Promise Packages" (p. 91).

Getting Started

As the children arrive, have them check in at the Adventure table, pick up their color-coded name tags, and meet their Small Group leaders. They can then proceed to work on the Life Application Project of their choice or move to the Bible Story Time with their Small Group leaders.

LIFE APPLICATION PROJECTS

Continue to offer ongoing projects, adding new ones as your schedule permits. (You can find more detailed information on pp. 84–104 on how to set up and work with the projects.) Consider any new projects that correlate with this week's lesson as noted in the Overview. Those projects will help kids experience activities that encourage them to accept others as Jesus does.

BIBLE STORY TIME

Gather the children together in a large group. They can sit within their Small Group families.

Weekly Activities

Welcome the children back to the Adventure. Proceed by making any necessary announcements, recognizing birthdays, or taking an offering.

Setting the Scene

Things You'll Need: Promise Path Factory Bible Time Machine with this week's Promise Path Action Topic, Conveyor Belt with this week's Promise Path Memory Verse, a whole canteloupe, a knife, a spoon, a bowl, a Slippery Road Ahead sign, and factory work clothes.

PREPARATION

Dress as a factory worker today. You will also need someone dressed up as a healed leper. This person will be hidden inside the Bible Time Machine. Provide a copy of the monologue in the Bible Story Presentation below.

Write this week's Promise Path Action Topic on a piece of paper large enough for kids to read. Then slip it into the Factory's Time Machine for use at the appropriate time during the session. Today's Promise Path Road Sign is the Slippery Road Ahead sign.

TOPIC INTRODUCTION

(Enter the Factory dressed as a factory worker.)

Hello! I'm glad to see you're all working on last week's Promise Path Action Topic—Get Involved at Church! Just by being here today, you're on the right path to following God's directions! I need a volunteer to come and help me get this week's Promise Path Action Topic out of our Bible Time Machine. (Allow a volunteer to pull this week's topic out of the machine.) Let's read it together. "Accept others as Jesus does." I bet most of you think you're already pretty accepting of others, and I hope you are. But sometimes it can get a little bit tricky. Let me show you what I mean. (Get out today's sign, Slippery Road Ahead, and show it to the group.)

Slippery Road Ahead. Hmmm, let's see if I can explain. I brought something to show you today. This is a canteloupe. (Show the group an uncut canteloupe.) Someone told me this is a really sweet, juicy, delicious fruit, but to tell you the truth, it doesn't necessarily look that way to me. The shell is rather crusty, the color is somewhat unattractive, and I can't even peel it with my fingers. So if I were in a grocery store shopping for fruit, I think I might pass up this canteloupe in favor of some green grapes or a nice red apple!

Since today's Promise Path Action Topic has to do with acceptance, I'm going to try to accept

64

this fruit. So let's cut it open and see what happens! (Cut open the fruit.) **Now look inside! I like the color much better! I like the texture better, too. Oh, but look at all these nasty looking seeds. I really don't know if I want to put up with them! What do you think?** (Let the kids respond.) **Okay, I'll clean out the middle.** (Scrape the seeds into a bowl with a spoon.) **Let's see what happens when I cut a slice and taste it.** (Cut a slice and take a taste.) **Mmm! It's delicious! If I hadn't taken the time to try to accept this fruit as one of the wonderful things that God created, I never would have gotten to know the delicious taste of this canteloupe!** (If you have enough canteloupe, give everyone a bite-size piece to try.)

Accepting other people is a lot like that. We can't just pay attention to the way someone looks on the outside. We have to get to know them on the inside, too! And we have to remember that everyone is different. Fruits come in different colors, sizes, textures, and with different things inside, just like people. And God wants us to accept people just the way they are. That's the way that God accepts us. That's the way Jesus accepted others, too.

(Pick up a piece of cut canteloupe and press it gently between your fingers until it slips out.) **Ooops! This is slippery! If I'm not careful, it will slip away from me! That reminds me of accepting others, too. Sometimes it takes a little effort to get to know others and get past how they look on the outside to find out how they are on the inside. Many times that effort will pay off, and we'll be thankful we didn't let the chance slip away! God wants us to keep on trying. God wants us to keep our hearts open to others. That's what it means to accept others like Jesus does.**

Today's story is about someone who had a hard time being accepted by others. Let's crank up our Bible Time Machine so we can go back to Bible times and find out why. (Turn on the Time Machine until the cleansed leper appears.)

Bible Story Presentation
Bible Basis: Mark 1:40–42
Storyteller: Healed leper

Things You'll Need: A Bible-time costume for the leper, also a very shabby coat or cape with holes and dirt. (You can find something in a resale shop.)

Today's story is a monologue by a healed leper. Mark tells us that the man came to Jesus and begged for his help, although Jesus' mission at that time was not to heal, but to preach. Jesus was so filled with compassion, however, that he touched the leper and made him well. Afterward, Jesus asked the man not to share his healing with anyone else so he would not be bombarded with others wanting to be healed. The man, however, was so filled with joy that he could not contain it, and he left telling many others what had happened.

The Healed Leper: Thank you for inviting me to your church today! I have a wonderful story I would like to share with you, a story I have shared with many others since a great thing happened in my life.

First, I want to ask you all a question. Have you ever felt unwanted, unloved, forgotten, left out, or unaccepted by others? *(Let the kids respond.)* So have I! There was a time in my life when no one wanted to come near me. No one wanted to have anything to do with me. And it was terrible! *(Put on the shabby coat.)*

How do you think it made me feel? *(Let the kids respond.)* It made me sad. It made me angry. I was very depressed and quite lonely. It was something that I would never wish on another person in the entire world.

You see, I was known as a leper, because I had a disease called leprosy. Leprosy is a nasty, contagious, skin disease. But as if having the disease wasn't bad enough, people back in Bible times thought that a person who had leprosy was an unclean person. Not only unclean on the outside, but on the inside, too! Have any of you ever known an illness to make someone bad on the inside? *(Shake your head no.)* Maybe a little crabby, but certainly not a bad person.

As a leper, I was required to separate myself from other people. I was not welcome to visit any of the places where healthy people were. I could not attend worship services or go to parties. I had to wear torn clothes, cover my face, and shout, "Unclean! Unclean!" so people would know I was coming near them. Some were so afraid of getting close that they threw rocks at me. No one could touch me because I might make them unclean, too.

I thought the rest of my life would be spent living with that terrible disease in great loneliness. And then one day I heard that Jesus was coming to a place near where I lived! Even though I knew I should have stayed away, I went to Jesus and got down on my knees and begged him! I said, "I know that you can heal me if you will."

Jesus didn't make me go away. I could tell that he was filled with love and compassion when he saw me. He reached out his hand and touched me—he actually touched me—and said, "I want to heal you. Be healed!" *(Throw off coat.)* Immediately the leprosy left my body, and I was cured! *(Look at "clean" hands and feet.)*

No one was afraid to be near me anymore. People talked to me, welcomed me, and accepted me. I was filled with so much joy that I told others my story, just like I'm telling you today. I made new friends. My entire life changed, and all because Jesus accepted me.

God wants us to accept others like Jesus does. Don't be afraid of what people look like or that they appear grouchy. Remember that even the people who don't appear to be nice on the outside *(indicate the shabby coat)*, were created by God. They may have lots of good things inside of them, if only someone gives them a chance to let them out!

Receiving the acceptance of others can change anyone. It can even change their appearance. You might see a very sad or angry face start to smile!

Comprehension Questions
Briefly discuss these questions with the children to clarify the main ideas in the Bible Story Presentation.
• **Why was today's visitor so sad and angry at one time in his life?** (Because he had a disease called leprosy. He wasn't allowed to be near other people, and no one would accept him.)
• **How did not being accepted make our visitor feel?** (Sad, angry, depressed, and lonely.)
• **What happened that changed the leper's life?** (He went to Jesus and asked for help. Jesus accepted him, touched him, and made him well.)
• **How did the leper's life change after Jesus helped him?** (He made new friends, was accepted by others, and was filled with joy.)
• **Why is it important to accept others like Jesus does?** (Because God wants us to. It can help others, make them feel better, and bring out the good inside of them.)

Promise Path Memory Verse
Things You'll Need: Promise Path Memory Verse (1 Samuel 16:7) written on a the scroll inside the Conveyor Belt, a bowl of ice cubes, and a small bowl of water.

I need a volunteer to help me crank up our Conveyor Belt to discover today's Promise Path Memory Verse. (Choose a volunteer and crank the lever of your Conveyor Belt until today's verse is showing.)

Let's read what it says. "God does not see the same way people see. People look at the outside of a person, but the Lord looks at the heart."

Jesus knew that the leper's heart was good. He looked beyond the outside of him and was willing to accept him. So he touched him and made him well. That changed the leper's entire life! Sometimes we see other people as unattractive, or grouchy, or mean. God wants us to get to know them better. God wants us to find out what they're like on the inside. We can do that by accepting others like Jesus does.

I've got something with me today that is very slippery when wet! It's an ice cube! I'm going to divide you into Small Groups. (Divide kids into their Small Groups, rows, or random circles.) **Next, I'm going to give each group a slippery ice cube. Try to pass the ice cube around the circle while you say each word of today's verse. But be careful, ice cubes are slippery when wet!**

Distribute ice cubes to each group. Dunk them briefly into a small bowl of water to make them slippery. Then kids must recite the verse one word at a time, as the cube is passed around their group. Continue until the ice cube is gone!

 If you choose to split the group in half, younger children can learn a shortened version of the verse—"People look at the outside of a person, but the Lord looks at the heart." 1 Samuel 16:7

LIFE APPLICATION SMALL GROUP TIME

Dismiss the children with their Small Group leaders, taking care to let the groups farthest away from the meeting area leave first. Each Small Group leader will need a copy of the Life Application page for today (p. 69). Be sure to give the page to leaders at least a week ahead of time so that they can be ready to work with their groups.

CHILDREN'S CHURCH WORSHIP

Things You'll Need: *Promise Kids Sing-along* cassette, audiocassette player, and an offering basket.

If you are using this section, be sure to allow kids a short time to stand up and stretch in between activities. You might also want to include some active songs during the singing time.

Singing
Choose music that fits the theme of this week's Promise Path Action Topic: Accept Others as Jesus Does. To reinforce this week's Promise Path Memory

Verse, teach the song "The Lord Looks at the Heart" on page 118 of this leader's guide. The song can be found on the *Promise Kids Sing-along* cassette. (See p. 128 for ordering information.)

Critter County Story
Through the familiar and friendly Critter County characters, the children can see this week's theme in action and be motivated to accept others as Jesus does. This week's story begins below.

Offering
One way children can learn to worship and respond to God is by giving. If you are using this curriculum for a children's church program, you may prefer to take the offering now instead of during the Weekly Activities portion of the Bible Story Time. Encourage children to think about other people who have accepted them as Jesus does as they thank God for something, either verbally or silently, when they pass the offering basket.

Praise and Prayer
Continue to help children through a prayer experience by offering them a line and asking them to repeat it. (Refer to Week 1, p. 32.) Encourage children to think about one way to accept others as Jesus does this week. Let the children conclude the prayer time with their own sentences, asking God to help them follow his directions.

MIDWEEK EXTRAS

Things You'll Need: *Promise Kids Sing-along* cassette; audiocassette player; a grocery bag or shopping bag for each team; a variety of empty grocery product containers such as a milk carton, detergent box, cereal box, canned goods, toothpaste box, shampoo bottle, and so on; index cards; tape; markers.

Game
ACCEPTANCE SHOPPING RELAY!
Divide kids into teams of six to ten kids. Give each team a shopping bag, a stack of index cards, tape, and a marker. At the opposite end of the room, set out a variety of empty grocery product containers. Because children will be running or walking fast (depending on your setting), an adult or older teen should give safety instructions and monitor the game.

One at a time, kids take their bag, race to the shopping area or "store," select an item, and return to the group. Then they take an index card and write

down one way to accept others or show acceptance of others. Team members can help. Children tape the card to the container, then return it to the store. Play continues until all of the containers proclaim ways to accept others and everyone has had at least one turn.

 ADJUSTMENT FOR YOUNGER AGES
Suggest that older children and younger children work together by having the younger children do the running, and the older children do the writing. Or you might write acceptance ideas onto the cards for the children, and just have children shop for the one they would like to work at this week.

If you have a group with no older children, leaders can do the writing, or the children can just verbally tell how they will accept others.

Singing
Singing is a fun way to praise God. Make use of the songs included in this book, beginning on page 105. Be sure to learn the song "The Lord Looks at the Heart" on page 118 of this leader's guide. The song can be found on the *Promise Kids Sing-along* cassette. And remember to include some active songs to give kids an opportunity to move around.

Critter County Story
THE GOLDEN RULER
"And now, boys and girls, the last Show 'n Tell speech will be given by Okey Dokey Donkey," said Mrs. Turtle, the teacher. As soon as she said the words, two of the boys in the back of the class began to whisper and snicker.

Rascal said, "Oh, get comfortable. It will take him forever and a day to say what's on his mind." Lunchbox laughed.

"His ears are so long and droopy, he'll probably trip on them, do a somersault and land on Mrs. Turtle's desk!" added Lunchbox.

Mrs. Turtle sensed what the boys were saying in the back of the room. She cleared her throat to get their attention and stared at them to let them know they should stop immediately.

During his Show 'n Tell speech, Okey Dokey talked about his grandmother. He told about her life and her ability to tell stories that had deep meaning. Many of her stories had helped Okey understand himself and the fact that he was different from some of his friends. He showed the scrapbook he had made for his grandmother. It was filled with pictures and notes of encouragement she had written to him. As he talked about her, Okey Dokey smiled from ear to ear as though he were talking about presents he had gotten on Christmas morning.

All the children in the class listened closely as he was telling his story. It was as though they were seeing a part of Okey that they had never seen before. His story showed the others why he liked himself and was so happy. If someone loves you as much as Okey's grandmother loved him, then it's easier to feel good about who you are.

It was lunchtime, and all the kids were just about finished eating. Rascal had almost finished eating his hot dog when suddenly he fell to the floor. Mrs. Turtle had gone out of the room to answer a phone call. Several of the critters could see that something was very wrong with Rascal. He was grabbing his throat, and his face was starting to turn blue.

"Maybe he's having a heart attack," yelled Beautiful the bunny.

"I think he's faking," said Petunia.

As soon as Okey Dokey took one look at Rascal, he knew immediately what was wrong and what to do. He walked as quickly as he could to get to Rascal. Then he reached over and picked up the raccoon and turned him so he was facing the other kids. After wrapping his arms around Rascal, Okey pulled and pushed on the top of his stomach. It seemed to hurt Rascal, and Lunchbox said, "Stop doing that, Okey. Stop. You'll hurt him."

But Rascal was still not breathing, so Okey did it again and again until finally . . . a piece of hot dog flew out of Rascal's mouth and landed on the floor.

Rascal took a deep breath and began to cry because he had been so scared.

All the kids were clapping and cheering Okey Dokey when Mrs. Turtle walked into the room. She heard about what had just happened and added her pats on the back for Okey.

Later that day at recess, Beautiful walked over to Okey. "Can I ask you something?" she said.

"Sure," was the quick response.

"When Rascal choked, why did you rush to help him? He has been so mean to you and has made fun of the way you talk and your long ears. Why were you so ready to help him?" asked Beautiful.

"Oh, it wasn't just me who helped Rascal; my grandmother and Jesus did also."

"What do you mean, Okey? You were the only one I saw," asked Beautiful.

Okey Dokey smiled that big, slow grin of his and slowly started to speak, "Well, it's like this. My grandmother always told me to keep a golden rule tucked in my pocket. She learned it from Jesus. The golden rule is: always treat others the way you want them to treat you. So it's easy to be kind and loving and to help others if I have that rule tucked in my pocket. In fact, I think I will spray-paint my ruler and make it gold. Then I will put it in my scrapbook to remind me of what my grandmother taught," said Okey.

And he did. On the ruler he printed, "Treat others the way you want them to treat you."

LIFE APPLICATION PAGE

For Small Group Leaders
• WEEK SIX •

- **Promise Path Action Topic:** Accept Others as Jesus Does
- **Desired Outcome:** That kids will make an effort to accept others, especially kids their own age. That they will also make a decision to put away put-downs toward others.
- **Bible Story:** Mark 1:40–42
- **Promise Path Memory Verse:** God does not see the same way people see. People look at the outside of a person, but the Lord looks at the heart. 1 Samuel 16:7 (ICB) (older children); People look at the outside of a person, but the Lord looks at the heart. 1 Samuel 16:7 (ICB) (younger children)

THINGS YOU'LL NEED

- Copy of "Tips for Small Group Leaders" (p. 21)
- *Bug Beepers for Promise Keepers* Critter County Activity Book (K–2)
- *Promise Kids on the Promise Path* Children's Journal (3–6)
- Promise Kids Prayer Poster
- Promise Path Action Topic Poster
- Newsprint
- Markers
- Chalkboard and chalk
- Three or four varieties of small, wrapped candies or gum

KID TALK

This week's Promise Path Action Topic focuses on accepting others as Jesus does. Begin your discussion by asking volunteers to share a story they have about feeling left out of something or being unaccepted. The stories can be about themselves or someone they know. Use these questions to further your discussion:
• **How do you think it feels not to be accepted?** (Scary, lonely, makes you angry, sad, disappointed.)
• **Why should we make the effort to accept others when we already have enough friends of our own?** (Encourage kids to take a moment to think about this before answering. Challenge kids to think of all kinds of people when answering, such as school kids, teachers, neighbors, doctors, store clerks, and so on.)
• **How can we be accepting to people we already know but don't like very much?** (Once again, ask kids to think creatively before rushing to an answer. Remind kids that today's theme doesn't say we have to like everybody, just accept them. We can do that by showing respect, giving people a fresh start or clean slate, accepting people's differences, or just

showing kindness because we care.)
• **How can we show our acceptance for people we don't know?** (Include families who move into the neighborhood, new kids at school or church, new teachers, and so on.)
• **What are put-downs and how can we put them away?** (Explain that put-downs are making fun of people, not giving them credit for anything they do, calling people names. We can get rid of put-downs by accepting people and what they do, and by standing up for someone who is being made fun of.)
• **Did anyone plan a new way to get involved at church this week?** (Let kids share their plans. Encourage kids who did not have a chance to do this, to try again this week.)
• **What did you learn in your Journal (or Activity Book) about getting involved at church?**
We all like to feel accepted. Jesus accepts us just the way we are. He wants us to accept others too!

GROUP-BUILDING ACTIVITY
(You may want to do this activity earlier in this session.)

If time permits, do the following group-building activity. Make sure an adult or older teen gives safety instructions and monitors the game. Put three or four varieties of small, wrapped candies into a bowl. Toss them into the air and let them spill on the ground. At the word *go*, let everyone run to pick up a piece. Kids then search to find someone else who picked up the same kind of candy as they did. After one or two other pieces have been found, that group can eat their candy while discussing one way to accept others this week. Play as long as desired.

PRAYER TALK

Start by asking: **Can you think of someone who needs to be accepted? Let's read our Promise Kids**

Prayer and then ask God to help us accept the person we just thought about.

Using the Promise Kids Prayer Poster, read the prayer together with your group. Encourage kids to finish the prayer by asking for God's help to be accepting toward others. Be sure to ask the group about any special prayer concerns, requests, or celebrations, and end by praying for each one.

SMALL GROUP TIP

As important as it is to be accepting of others, you may get questioned about the topic of "stranger danger."

Assure kids that whatever they have been taught to stay safe is surely in keeping with this week's theme. While God wants us to be accepting of others, he is not asking us to put ourselves at risk. Focus on the numerous opportunities to be accepting of others while in the presence of parents, teachers, and other friends. Showing kindness and friendship to kids at school, new neighbors, and the grocery store cashier will be plenty for young people to handle.

WEEK SEVEN OVERVIEW

- **Promise Path Action Topic:** Make a Difference in the World
- **Desired Outcome:** That kids will make a decision to do an act of kindness in their neighborhood or school without someone's having to know about it.
- **Bible Story:** Matthew 5:13–16
- **Promise Path Memory Verse:** You should be a light for other people. Live so that they will see the good things you do. Live so that they will praise your Father in heaven. Matthew 5:16 (ICB) (older children); You should be a light for other people. Matthew 5:16 (ICB) (younger children)
- **Bible Story Presentation:** A fictional witness to the Sermon on the Mount will tell the story.
- **Life Application Projects:** The Life Application Projects that correlate with the Promise Path Action Topic for Week 7 are "Promise Path Planes" (p. 101), "Promise Path Lamps or Candles" (p. 87), "Promise Path Research" (p. 94), and "Make a Difference Gift Cards" (p. 103).

Getting Started

As the children arrive, have them check in at the Adventure table, pick up their color-coded name tags, and meet their Small Group leaders. They can then proceed to work on the Life Application Project of their choice or move to the Bible Story Time with their Small Group leaders.

LIFE APPLICATION PROJECTS

Continue to offer ongoing projects, adding new ones as your schedule permits. (You can find more detailed information on pp. 84–104 on how to set up and work with the projects.) Consider any new projects that correlate with this week's lesson as noted in the Overview. Those projects will help kids experience activities that encourage them to make a difference in their world.

BIBLE STORY TIME

Gather the children together in a large group. They can sit within their Small Group families.

Weekly Activities

Welcome the children back to the Adventure. Proceed by making any necessary announcements, recognizing birthdays, or taking an offering.

Setting the Scene

Things You'll Need: Promise Path Factory Bible Time Machine with this week's Promise Path Action Topic, Conveyor Belt with this week's Promise Path Memory Verse, poster board, a Walk sign, and factory work clothes.

PREPARATION

Dress as a factory worker today. You will also need someone dressed up as a witness who heard the Sermon on the Mount. This person will be hidden inside the Bible Time Machine. Provide a copy of the monologue in the Bible Story Presentation below.

Write this week's Promise Path Action Topic on a piece of paper large enough for kids to read. Then slip it into the Factory's Bible Time Machine for use at the appropriate time during the session. You will also need to make a poster illustrating the four points for "walking in the direction of making a difference," found in the Topic Introduction below. Today's Promise Path Road Sign is the Walk sign.

TOPIC INTRODUCTION

(Enter the Factory dressed as a factory worker.)

Hello! How many of you practiced accepting others like Jesus does last week? (Let kids respond.) **That's great! We're back to work on another Promise Path Action Topic, and I'll need a volunteer to get this week's topic out of the Bible Time Machine.** (Allow a volunteer to pull this week's topic out of the machine.) **Let's read it together. "Make a difference in the world." Wow! That's a big goal, and something I hope we all have a chance to do.**

Let me show you today's road sign so we can play a short game that will help us get started on making a difference in the world. (Show the Walk sign to the children.) **Walk! What does walking do?** (Let the kids respond.) **Walking gets us places. It requires an effort, and a reaching out, even if it's only to get across the room! If we're going to make a difference in the world, we're going to have to make an effort to reach out. And we have to be alert so that we can follow these four points that will walk us in the direction of making a difference. First: See the places you can go; Second: Watch carefully to see where you're going; Third: Proceed with caution so it's worth your effort; and Fourth: Reach your goal by getting there!** (Illustrate these points with the poster you made before the session began.)

Everyone please stand up. (Wait while everyone stands up.) I'm going to read a short story. As long as I'm following the four steps I've written on this poster, I want you to walk in place. Whenever you think I'm not following one of the four steps, I want you to stop. Let's see where we end up going!

(Walk in place.) Once upon a time, Nancy and Bill decided they wanted to make a difference in their world. But they wondered how to go about it. After a while the kids got too busy with school, and they put off making a difference in their world. (Stop walking!) But then their mom and dad encouraged them to try again, and they began looking into different possibilities. (Start walking again.) How could they do something good in their world? One way was to spend a Saturday afternoon helping hungry people at a food pantry. Another possibility was to set up a lemonade stand so they could make money to give to their church's missionaries. They also discovered that there were people in some countries who didn't even own a Bible, and Nancy and Bill thought perhaps they could buy some Bibles from a used book store and send them to kids around the world. In fact, there were so many chances to make a difference that they felt overwhelmed and couldn't decide on anything at all! (Stop walking.) One day, Mom told Nancy and Bill about a small boy who had no one to take care of him at the hospital where she worked. He had been abandoned by everyone he loved, and he'd never heard about Jesus. That gave Nancy and Bill an idea. (Start walking again.) They decided to volunteer some time at the hospital caring for and playing with children who didn't have someone there all the time to love them. Both Nancy and Bill were excited about their decision—until they talked to other hospital workers and found out that volunteers were only allowed to work with children at certain times of the day. That meant Nancy and Bill would have to give up in-line skating after school. And they loved to skate! It was a tough decision. (Stop walking!) They thought about it and thought about it. Then they talked about how much Jesus gave up for them. He was willing to die for their sins! (Start walking again.) They decided to give up their skating time to play with the kids at the hospital instead. Nancy and Bill found a lot of new friends. They made a difference in the lives of many children!

(Have the children sit down.) Making a difference means making choices, making a commitment,

and following through. Today's story is about someone in Bible times who had the opportunity to hear Jesus teach how people can make a difference. Jesus' talk is called the Sermon on the Mount. (Turn on the Bible Time Machine until your witness appears.)

Bible Story Presentation
Bible Basis: Matthew 5:13–16
Storyteller: Jude (or Judith), a village baker who attended the Sermon on the Mount

Things You'll Need: A Bible-time costume and baker's hat or apron for Jude; a Matzoh (or very plain, unsalted cracker) and a Saltine (or more salty cracker) for each child; a candle and matches; a miniature cupcake, muffin, donut hole, or cookie for each child if possible

Today's story is a monologue by Jude, a baker from Cana who witnessed the Sermon on the Mount. Set up a small table to hold the crackers and candle (and the sweets, if you are using them). This should be out of children's reach but somewhere well in sight.

Jude: Good day to you! My name is Jude (or Judith), and I am one of the premier bakers in Galilee! People come to our market in Cana from miles around to buy my bread and sweetcakes. Yes, people come from even as far as Nazareth to taste my goods.

The children especially love to come to my market stand. Oh, how I love children! Their faces shine when they taste the things I've baked. But you know, I haven't always liked children. When the children crowded around my stand, the grownups couldn't get through. And the grownups were the ones with all the money! So I'd try to scatter the children from the front of my stand (*motioning as if shooing children in front of the table*): "Scram! Go away!" I would yell at them.

Early one morning, I was surprised to find that no one showed up at the Cana market. "What's going on?" I asked the farmer who was packing up his stand across from mine.

He said, "Jesus of Nazareth is teaching on Mount Tabor, not too far away. It seems many of the villagers from Nazareth and Cana have gone to the mountain to listen to him."

Jesus! I remembered him. Not long before, he had turned water into wine at my cousin Simon's wedding!

Well, I wasn't going to miss this great event. If the crowds of people didn't come to the market to buy my bread, I would just have to take the bread to them. I packed up the morning's work (*making motions to illustrate*), loaded it into a basket, strapped the basket on my back, and walked the long way to Mount Tabor.

I arrived around noon—just in time for lunch. How hungry the people were, and oh, was I happy to see the money pouring in for all the bread and sweetcakes I sold. But then Jesus began to speak, and everyone got very quiet.

He was such a nice teacher—and always so gentle and happy. He began to paint pictures for us. No, not pictures with paint, of course. But with his words!

He said, "You are the salt of the earth." Isn't that interesting? Being a baker, I know that salt does all kinds of wonderful things. It preserves food and keeps it from harm, but most of all it makes my baking taste better.

Here, let's try an experiment. (*Give one unsalted cracker to each child. You may need to have other adults or teens help you.*) This is a cracker with no salt. Let's taste it and see how we like it. (*Wait for the kids to taste the plain cracker; they needn't eat it all if they'd rather not.*) It's not bad, but it's not especially tasty. Now let's try a different kind of cracker—one with salt on it. (*Give each child a salted cracker and lead them in taking a bite.*) Mmm. That tastes a bit better, doesn't it?

Yep, I know from my years of baking that a little bit of salt keeps food from being harmful and makes things taste much better! So when Jesus said we are the salt of the earth, he meant we try to keep people safe and make every person and situation better.

Jesus painted another word picture for us on that mountain. He said, "You should be a light for other people. Live so that they will see the good things you do. Live so that they will praise your Father in heaven."

Now I, for one, am awfully thankful for light. Do you know, I have to get up at four o'clock in the morning to do all the baking for the day? You see, the market opens at seven, and if I missed it, what would folks do without fresh-baked bread and sweetcakes?

I don't know if you've ever noticed, but it's very dark at four o'clock in the morning. (*Turn off most of the overhead lights in the room.*) So when I get up to bake bread, the first thing I do is light a candle. (*Light the candle set on the table.*) Then I can see just enough to knead dough for my bread. Doesn't that little bit of light help a whole lot? And don't you feel relieved that it isn't so dark anymore? Now, imagine if we had as many lights as there are people in this room—if everyone acted like a light. (*Turn the overhead lights back on.*) Why, how much brighter and cheerier it would be! I think that's what Jesus meant—be bright and cheery and helpful to the whole world.

On my way home, I thought about how I could be salt and light in the town of Cana. And I remembered how Jesus was so kind to the children. That's the way he was with all the people: happy, gentle, helpful, and always praising God.

The next day, I got up at *three* o'clock in the morning. I lit my candle and began to bake. I'd decided to bring light to all the children who came to my market stand that day. I wanted to be like salt—to make everything seem better! I would do something good to make people happy, just as they were around Jesus. Can you guess what I did? I gave away free sweetcakes! To every child! And just like Jesus said, I made sure I praised God the Father in heaven as I gave them away. Friday

Now every Sunday people flock to Cana's market from miles around. Why? It's not just because I'm one of the premier bakers in the region! It's because I try to make a difference in people's lives. You see, I've found a way to be salt and light to the world, just like Jesus said. Praise God! (*If you have treats to give to the children, repeat this to every child as you give a "sweetcake" to him or her. If the child says thank you, say, "Thank God!"*)

Comprehension Questions
Briefly discuss these questions with the children to clarify the main ideas in the Bible Story Presentation.
• **What word pictures did Jesus use to tell us what we are like?** (Salt and light.)
• **What does salt do?** (Preserves food and keeps it from harm. Makes food taste better.)
• **Why did Jesus say we should be like salt?** (We should try to keep people safe and make every situation better.)
• **What did Jesus mean when he said we are the light of the world?** (We help people and make things brighter and cheerier.)
• **How did Jude (or Judith) the baker try to be like salt and light?** (The baker learned to love children and brought happiness to people by giving the children free treats.)

Promise Path Memory Verse
Things You'll Need: Promise Path Memory Verse (Matthew 5:16) written on a the scroll inside of the Conveyor Belt.

I need a volunteer to help me crank up our Conveyor Belt to discover today's Promise Path Memory Verse. (Choose a volunteer and crank the lever of your Conveyor Belt until today's verse is showing.)

Let's read what it says. "You should be a light for other people. Live so that they will see the

good things you do. Live so that they will praise your Father in heaven." Being a light for others means our actions should shine out and speak louder than words. We can do that by being the salt of the earth and a light to others, like we just talked about. Jesus needs us to be his salt and his light so that we can shine brightly in everything that we do. So when people look at us, they should be able to say, "He or she must be a child of God!" What are some things we can do to shine for Jesus? (Let kids respond. Answers might include go to church, be loving, sharing, caring, helpful, reach out to others, and spread the word of God.)

If we're going to be God's light in the world, our actions are going to have to shine. Let's learn today's verse by coming up with actions that represent different words in the verse. For example, what action can we make instead of saying the word *light*? (Let the kids come up with an action like spreading their hands out wide beside their face.) We'll say the verse again, but this time we'll insert that action instead of saying the word. (Say the verse, inserting the action in place of the word. Then repeat the above steps, substituting another action for another word. Do this until the verse is filled with action and the kids have it memorized.)

 If you choose to split the group in half, younger children can learn a shortened version of the verse—"You should be a light for other people." Matthew 5:16

LIFE APPLICATION SMALL GROUP TIME

Dismiss the children with their Small Group leaders, taking care to let the groups farthest away from the meeting area leave first. Each Small Group leader will need a copy of the Life Application page for today (p. 76). Be sure to give the page to leaders at least a week ahead of time so that they can be ready to work with their groups.

CHILDREN'S CHURCH WORSHIP

Things You'll Need: *Promise Kids Sing-along* cassette, audiocasette player, and an offering basket.

If you are using this section, be sure to allow kids a short time to stand up and stretch in between activities. You might also want to include some active songs during the singing time.

Singing
Choose music that fits the theme of this week's Promise Path Action Topic: Make a Difference in the World. To reinforce this week's Promise Path Memory Verse, teach the song "Be a Light" on page 120 of this leader's guide. The song can be found on the *Promise Kids Sing-along* cassette. (See p. 128 for ordering information.)

Critter County Story
Through the familiar and friendly Critter County characters, the children can see this week's theme in action and be motivated to make a difference in the world. This week's story begins on page 75.

Offering
One way children can learn to worship and respond to God is by giving. If you are using this curriculum for a children's church program, you may prefer to take the offering now instead of during the Weekly Activities portion of the Bible Story Time. Encourage children to think about the world God made as they thank him for something, either verbally or silently, when they pass the offering basket.

Praise and Prayer
Continue to help children through a prayer experience by offering them a line and asking them to repeat it. (Refer to Week 1, p. 32.) Encourage children to think about one way to make a difference in the world this week. Let the children conclude the prayer time with their own sentences, asking God to help them follow his directions.

MIDWEEK EXTRAS

Things You'll Need: *Promise Kids Sing-along* cassette, audiocassette player, signs and props to accompany tasks (see below).

Game
MAKE A DIFFERENCE OLYMPICS!
Set up a variety of different stations around the room. Label each station with general ways kids can make a difference in the world. (For example: caring, helping, giving, sharing, and teaching.) Under the label, write a task that kids must do while coming up with one way to make a difference that fits the label at that station. Tasks can be: doing jumping jacks; slapping knees, then clapping hands; snapping fingers; doing sit-ups; jumping rope; and so on. (For example: At the "Teaching" station, while jumping

rope, a child may say, "I will tell my friends about Jesus and invite them to my church.")

Ask a leader to stand at each station to make sure that kids follow the correct task while coming up with one way to make a difference in the world. As soon as children finish at one station, they can move on to another. If desired, let kids time themselves to see how quickly they can accomplish the Make a Difference Olympics!

 ADJUSTMENT FOR YOUNGER AGES
Suggest that older children and younger children work together in teams. Older children can read the directions for younger kids, and both of them can work together to come up with a way to make a difference, while doing the station task.

If you have only younger children in your group, tell them what to do at each station. Then help them think of a way to make a difference in the world.

Singing

Singing is a fun way to praise God. Make use of the songs included in this book, beginning on page 105. Be sure to learn the song "Be a Light" on page 120 of this leader's guide. The song can be found on the *Promise Kids Sing-along* cassette. And remember to include some active songs to give kids an opportunity to move around.

Critter County Story

AT HOME IN MY HEART

"Lunchbox, are you going to go on the kids' club trip this weekend?" asked Rascal. "I heard Pastor Penguin say they are planning to take us to a homeless shelter in a nearby town. Wonder what it will be like."

"I don't know. I guess it will just be feeding a bunch of people who are poor—outside if they don't have homes. At least they don't have to clean their room."

"That wasn't very nice, Lunchbox," said Beautiful the bunny. "Those people have feelings, too. They can't help it that their fathers or mothers don't have jobs and can't afford to have a nice place to live."

Rascal spoke up. "I'm just afraid if we go there on Saturday that we will catch some bad disease or something. Or maybe they will rob us."

Again, Beautiful was sad because of the things that were being said. "Rascal, you won't get sick from being there helping those people, and they aren't bad or evil. They just don't have all of the things that you and I do. But one thing they do have is feelings, and we need to go there and show love and kindness."

When the weekend came, everyone loaded up the Critter County bus, and before long, they found the shelter where all the people had gathered. "Liona

Lou, why don't you and the kids unload all of the food we brought, and Sydney and I will get the clothing and other gifts," suggested Lester.

"That sounds good to me," answered Liona as she and the boys carried in turkey, beans, and potatoes. The younger critters' eyes were as big as plates when they walked into the room and saw a number of poor men, women, and children waiting for them.

"Here, let us help," offered one of the men. And all of them went out to the bus to help the folks from Critter County unload and get set up.

Lunchbox leaned over to Rascal as they lifted a box together and said, "These people are really nice to offer to help us like that." Beautiful overheard what Lunchbox said and smiled to herself.

Liona Lou and the kitchen staff served a wonderful dinner. The people who ate it were all smiles and hugs as the food was passed. Everyone ate until they were so full they couldn't even wiggle.

After dinner, Sydney went up to the microphone. "Ladies and gentlemen, boys and girls. We are so glad to be here with you all today." He no more had the words out of his mouth when all of the people started clapping and cheering as their way of thanking the group from Critter County. Sydney was so moved by the outpouring of gratitude and love that he had a tear in his eye. Finally, he was able to speak again, "And now we have brought some things we would like to leave with you."

All the Critter County folks handed out coats, blankets, and extra food to the people who needed them. Soon the boxes were empty, but the hearts were full. About the time the Critter County crew was ready to clean up and get back on the bus to go home, one of the men walked to the microphone.

"We'd like to thank all of you wonderful folks for coming our way. You have given us hope that someday everything will be better for us. Thank you. And now we have a little gift for you to take home." And he handed Sydney a box of letters, notes, and cards.

All the way home, the critters on the bus opened and read the notes of thanks that the people had written. Some had drawn and colored pictures. Others had written poetry. Each had words of deepest thanks.

Finally, as the bus pulled back into Critter County, Rascal leaned over to Lunchbox. "You know what?" he said. "I went to that place thinking I was going to give those people some food and clothes and stuff. And instead, I am coming back home feeling like they gave me far more than we took to them."

Lunchbox nodded his head. "This is the best feeling I've had in a long time. I'm going to go home and fix my bike and take it next time. Some of the boys might like to have it," he said with a smile on his face and in his heart.

LIFE APPLICATION PAGE

For Small Group Leaders
• WEEK SEVEN •

- **Promise Path Action Topic:** Make a Difference in the World
- **Desired Outcome:** That kids will make a decision to do an act of kindness in their neighborhood or school without someone's having to know about it.
- **Bible Story:** Matthew 5:13–16
- **Promise Path Memory Verse:** You should be a light for other people. Live so that they will see the good things you do. Live so that they will praise your Father in heaven. Matthew 5:16 (ICB) (older children); You should be a light for other people. Matthew 5:16 (ICB) (younger children)

THINGS YOU'LL NEED

- Copy of "Tips for Small Group Leaders" (p. 21)
- *Bug Beepers for Promise Keepers* Critter County Activity Book (K–2)
- *Promise Kids on the Promise Path* Children's Journal (3–6)
- Promise Kids Prayer Poster
- Promise Path Action Topic Poster
- Newsprint
- Markers
- Chalkboard and chalk

KID TALK

This week's Promise Path Action Topic focuses on making a difference in the world. This topic may be overwhelming for some children, especially those just coming into the church. Remind children that they can make a difference in very small ways that will please God, too! Begin your discussion by asking these questions:

- **Why is it so important that we all try to make a difference in the world?** (The world is a big place! God wants everyone to reach out to light the way for others!)
- **How can making a difference help God?** (We are Jesus' disciples. It's up to us to care for others and spread God's Word.)
- **How can we make a difference in the world when we're young?** (Encourage kids to think of a variety of different ways to reach out with the Good News and help others. Make a list of their ideas on the board or newsprint.)
- **How can we show others that we are God's light?** (Our actions should show others that we are children of God. Our words should help teach others about Jesus and invite others into God's family.)

- **Did you show your acceptance for others last week? How?** (Let kids share their stories of acceptance. Celebrate what they did and encourage them to continue.)
- **What did you learn in your Journal (or Activity Book) about accepting others?**

Even though you're young, there are many ways you can make a difference in God's world. It starts by the little things you do every day, and it can grow into bigger things that you plan to accomplish in the future.

GROUP-BUILDING ACTIVITY

(You may want to do this activity earlier in the session.)

If time permits, do the following group-building activity. Ask everyone to sit in a circle. One person begins by saying his or her name and one way he or she will try to make a difference in the world, accompanied by movement. The action can be anything and does not have to relate to the statement. For example: "My name is Brenda, and I'm going to write to our missionary in Africa." Brenda says this while touching one finger to her nose.

The next person repeats what the previous person said and did, and then adds his or her own statement and action. Play continues around the circle until everyone can repeat everyone else's plan and action.

PRAYER TALK

Let's begin our prayer today by remembering that our words and actions can light up the world for Jesus! It's up to us to make a difference in God's world. Let's read our Promise Kids Prayer and then tell God one way we came up with to make a difference in the world this week. Using the Promise Kids Prayer Poster, read the prayer together with your group. Encourage kids to finish the prayer, if they're comfortable, by telling God one way they will try to make a difference in the world this week. Be sure to ask the group about any special prayer concerns, requests, or celebrations, and end by praying for each one.

SMALL GROUP TIP

Some children, especially newcomers, may feel uncomfortable reaching out with the Good News so soon after coming into God's family. Even if they are excited about Jesus, they may feel unprepared to tell others or invite others in. Remind these children that being a child of God is not measured by the amount of knowledge we have. Instead, it's showing others God's love by our actions, the everyday things we do, and sharing our excitement about Jesus. Even the newest member in God's family can be a light in the world by showing love, kindness, and respect for others. Encourage these children to make a difference in other people's lives by starting with easy-to-accomplish goals. For example, children can make a difference in their family's life by being more helpful at home. After that's mastered, they might try to make a difference at school by helping the teacher or kids who missed school due to illness. Finally, children can come up with a way to reach out to the world and make a difference by writing a letter to a missionary kid, getting involved in a fund-raiser for a local outreach, or working with others to accomplish a greater goal.

WEEK EIGHT OVERVIEW

- **Promise Path Action Topic:** Stay on the Promise Path
- **Desired Outcome:** That kids will identify one thing to work on that will help them stay on the Promise Path.
- **Bible Story:** Matthew 28:1–10
- **Promise Path Memory Verse:** You will teach me God's way to live. Being with you will fill me with joy. At your right hand I will find pleasure forever. Psalm 16:11 (ICB) (older children); You will teach me God's way to live. Psalm 16:11 (ICB) (younger children)
- **Bible Story Presentation:** A Resurrection drama
- **Life Application Projects:** The Life Application Projects that correlate with the Promise Path Action Topic for Week 8 are "Promise Path Parade" (p. 86), "Bible-time Drama" (p. 98), and "Topographical Promise Path" (p. 94).

Getting Started

As the children arrive, have them check in at the Adventure table, pick up their color-coded name tags, and meet their Small Group leaders. They can then proceed to work on the Life Application Project of their choice or move to the Bible Story Time with their Small Group leaders.

LIFE APPLICATION PROJECTS

Continue to offer ongoing projects, adding new ones as your schedule permits. Any new projects you add need to be short ones you can finish this week unless you plan to extend your Adventure. (You can find more detailed information on pp. 84–104 on how to set up and work with the projects.)

BIBLE STORY TIME

Gather the children together in a large group. They can sit within their Small Group families.

Weekly Activities

Welcome the children back to the Adventure. Proceed by making any necessary announcements, recognizing birthdays, or taking an offering.

Setting the Scene

Things You'll Need: Promise Path Factory Bible Time Machine with this week's Promise Path Action Topic, Conveyor Belt with this week's Promise Path Memory Verse, poster board, a blindfold, a Yield sign, and factory work clothes.

PREPARATION

Dress as a factory worker today. You will also need several people dressed up as Bible-time characters for the Resurrection drama. These people will be

hidden off stage. If needed, provide a copy of the script found in the Bible-time Drama project on page 98 for the Bible Story Presentation below.

Write this week's Promise Path Action Topic on a piece of paper large enough for kids to read. Then slip it into the Factory's Time Machine for use at the appropriate time during the session. Today's Promise Path Road Sign is the Yield sign.

TOPIC INTRODUCTION

(Enter the factory dressed as a factory worker.)

Hello! Welcome to our last day together in the Promise Path Factory. Has everyone had a good time working on following God's directions? (Let kids respond.) Great! I hope you'll enjoy your future on the Promise Path!

I need a volunteer to get this week's topic out of the Bible Time Machine. (Allow a volunteer to pull this week's topic out of the machine.) Let's read it together. "Stay on the Promise Path." What great advice. We've done a lot of work learning how to follow God's directions every day of our life. And we didn't do it just for eight weeks. These are habits we want to make last for a lifetime! They're decisions that will help you Promise Kids grow up to be promise keepers. That's what staying on the Promise Path means.

Today's sign is the Yield sign. Does anyone know what the road sign "yield" means? (Let kids respond.) When we yield, we slow down so that we can look around and see what's happening. So what in the world does that have to do with staying on the Promise Path? (Let kids respond.) As we go through life, we have to constantly be aware of what's going on around us. We have to think about how our actions will affect others, and whether or not our actions are following God's directions. Let me show you what I mean.

(Put a blindfold on at this time. Then wander around the room, bumping into things, and looking lost. Be cautious not to hurt yourself! Then take the blindfold off.) **Whew! That was a little scary! When I'm not looking to see where I'm going or what I'm doing, just about anything can happen! I can get hurt, or I could hurt someone else. But when my eyes are wide open and I take the time to yield and look before I act, then I can proceed with caution and care, making sure that what I'm doing is best for me and everyone else around me.**

If we're going to stay on the Promise Path, we need to remember to yield every day. It's important to plan what we're going to do and make sure that we're always following God's directions.

We have a special presentation for our Bible story today. Let's turn on our Bible Time Machine for the last time to take us back to Bible days. (Turn on the Time Machine until your characters appear.)

Bible Story Presentation

Bible Basis: Matthew 28:1–10
Characters: Mary Magdalene, the other Mary, guards, angel, Jesus

Things You'll Need: Bible-time costumes for your drama characters. Today's story is the drama that was offered as a Life Application Project (p. 98).

If you did not offer this project, you will need to:
• present the drama found on that page, using the script provided;
• present the drama as a dramatic story, using a narrator to tell the story while several actors mime the movement; or
• adapt the drama as a monologue by someone who witnessed the action that took place.

Suggestions for costumes, set decoration, and props are found in the project notes.

If you offered the Promise Path Parade project on page 86, you may wish to conclude your Bible Time Presentation with the Promise Path Parade.

Comprehension Questions

Briefly discuss these questions with the children to clarify the main ideas in the Bible Story Presentation.
• **What happened when the women went to the tomb?** (There was an earthquake, a stone was rolled away from the tomb, and an angel appeared.)
• **What did the angel say to the women?** (The angel told them not to be afraid. He knew they were looking for Jesus, and told them that Jesus was not there, but had risen. The angel told them to look inside the tomb and then go and tell others what they had heard and seen.)
• **What did the women do after they saw that Jesus was not there?** (They hurried away, afraid but filled with joy, to tell Jesus' disciples.)
• **Who did the women meet when running to tell the disciples?** (Jesus)
• **What did Jesus say to the women?** (He greeted them and told them not to be afraid. Then Jesus told the women to tell his disciples to go to Galilee where they too would see him.)

Promise Path Memory Verse

Things You'll Need: Promise Path Memory Verse (Psalm 16:11) written on a the scroll inside the Conveyor Belt. You will also need balloons and markers.

I need a volunteer to help me crank up our Conveyor Belt to discover today's Promise Path Memory Verse. (Choose a volunteer and crank the lever of your Conveyor Belt until today's verse is showing.)

Let's read what it says. "You will teach me God's way to live. Being with you will fill me with joy. At your right hand I will find pleasure forever." Jesus did teach us how to live. And we've been learning how to live as his Promise Kids. That will bring us closer to God and fill our lives with joy!

Let's review some of the Promise Path Action Topics. They teach us how to live the way God wants us to, by following his directions. (Take a few minutes to review your Promise Path Action Topics.) **Great job! Let's celebrate by blowing up Bible verse balloons!**

(Distribute at least one balloon to every child. Blow them up. Divide kids into groups of thirteen. Then write two words of today's Bible verse on each balloon. Have kids arrange themselves in order of the words of the Promise Path Memory Verse. Ask one child to pop his or her balloon. Then see if the kids can say the verse, remembering the words written on the balloon that was popped. Proceed by popping another balloon and repeating the verse. Continue until all the balloons are popped and the verse is memorized.)

 If you choose to split the group in half, younger children can learn a shortened version of the verse—"You will teach me God's way to live." Psalm 16:11

LIFE APPLICATION
SMALL GROUP TIME

Dismiss the children with their Small Group leaders, taking care to let the groups farthest away from the meeting area leave first. Each Small Group leader will need a copy of the Life Application page for today (p. 82). Be sure to give the page to leaders at least a week ahead of time so that they can be ready to work with their groups.

CHILDREN'S CHURCH WORSHIP

Things You'll Need: *Promise Kids Sing-along* cassette, audiocasette player, and an offering basket.

If you are using this section, be sure to allow kids a short time to stand up and stretch in between activities. You might also want to include some active songs during the singing time.

Singing

Choose music that fits the theme of this week's Promise Path Action Topic: Stay on the Promise Path. To reinforce this week's Promise Path Memory Verse, teach the song "Show Me, O God" on page 123 of this leader's guide. The song can be found on the *Promise Kids Sing-along* cassette. (See p. 128 for ordering information.)

Critter County Story

Through the familiar and friendly Critter County characters, the children can see this week's theme in action and be motivated to stay on the Promise Path. This week's story begins on page 81.

Offering

One way children can learn to worship and respond to God is by giving. If you are using this curriculum for a children's church program, you may prefer to take the offering now instead of during the Weekly Activities portion of the Bible Story Time. Encourage children to think about all the things they've learned during their 50-Day Adventure as they thank God for something, either verbally or silently, when they pass the offering basket.

Praise and Prayer

Continue to help children through a prayer experience by offering them a line and asking them to repeat it. (Refer to Week 1, p. 32.) This week, encour-

age children to think about one way to stay on the Promise Path in the weeks ahead. Let the children conclude the prayer time with their own sentences, asking God to help them follow his directions.

MIDWEEK EXTRAS

Things You'll Need: Write the word *Promise* in large letters and photocopy it on card stock so that every child will have two copies. You will also need markers, the *Promise Kids Sing-along* cassette, and an audiocasette player.

Game
STAY ON THE PROMISE PATH MATCH-UP!

Divide kids into groups of eight. Give each child two sheets of card stock with the word *Promise* written on them. Ask each child to write one of the eight Promise Path Action Topics onto the back of each card. Then collect them and mix them up. Lay them out on the floor, face down, so that only the word *Promise* can be seen. Create a 4' x 4' square.

Let kids take turns flipping over two cards, trying to create Promise Path matches. If a match is not made, those cards are turned back face down. If a match is made, the cards are kept by the player. The next player takes a turn, trying to get a match. Continue the play until all matches are obtained. The children might race with another group, if desired.

ADJUSTMENT FOR YOUNGER AGES
Suggest that older children and younger children work together in teams. Younger kids may also wish to color Promise Path pictures to match instead of writing the topic out in words.

Singing

Singing is a fun way to praise God. Make use of the songs included in this book, beginning on page 105. Be sure to learn the song "Show Me, O God" on page 123 of this leader's guide. The song can be found on the *Promise Kids Sing-along* cassette. And remember to include some active songs to give kids an opportunity to move around.

Critter County Story

SMARTER THAN A FOX

There is a dark and evil character who lurks around the edges of Critter County. He is to be feared and avoided. He seems harmless enough at first meeting because he is so charming. Do not be fooled.

Although he tries to get the critters and children to play with and follow him, that always leads to trouble. He is a fox whose name is Funco. Being with him may be fun, but it is always dangerous. His purpose is to keep critters and kids off the Promise Path that leads to happiness and obedience.

No one in the County knows this truth any better than the critters who have lived there for some time. Rascal was one of the first to meet this fox, and he will never forget it. He had been told by his parents to come straight home from baseball practice. Funco was sitting by the edge of the woods and whispered, "Come with me, Rascal. We'll have some fun scaring kids from behind the trees in the woods. And you can take the shortcut and get home in time."

So Rascal followed him deep into the woods. They scared some kids all right, but Rascal was the one who ended up terrified when he fell into a deep hole and hurt his leg. His parents, the fire department, and most everyone else was looking for him. Finally, God answered all their prayers and Rascal was discovered by the bug beepers, who found the hole. Their alarm sounds alerted everyone, and help was on the way.

Lunchbox heard the whispers of Funco in school one day. The kids were taking a test, and Lunchbox didn't know the answers. Funco sat down in the seat behind him and said softly, "Look in your notebook. The answers are right there on top. Nobody will see you looking, and you'll get an *A*." Well, Lunchbox listened to the fox this time instead of to God. And just as he opened his notebook to get the answers,

Mrs. Penguin looked around the room and saw what Lunchbox was doing. He had to stay after school every day for a week and clean desks and do other work. The hardest part was telling his parents what he had done and seeing the disappointment on their faces. "Don't worry, Mom and Dad, I promise you that I will never do that again." And he has kept his promise.

Sydney the squirrel has a different tale to tell. Whenever Funco comes up to the smart squirrel, Sydney makes a wise decision. He walks away because he knows that Funco will try to get him to leave the Promise Path. Sydney knows that the ol' fox is always up to no good. He always wants to make others do bad things.

One day when Sydney was teaching Sunday school, he was telling everyone in his class about the promise key chain he had made.

"You see, boys and girls, I want to always travel in the right direction. I want to go the right way and not get lost. Bad things can happen when you go down the wrong road by making unwise choices. So I decided to make a key chain, and I painted this verse on it."

Sydney held up the key chain and began to slowly write these words on the blackboard: "You will teach me God's way to live" (Psalm 16:11). And then Sydney explained, "I wish I had room for the rest of the verse, 'Being with you will fill me with joy. At your right hand I will find pleasure forever.'"

The lovable little squirrel with the big, brown eyes smiled at the boys and girls. "God promises to teach us the best way to live. Staying on the Promise Path and obeying him can bring us happiness and keep us safe. If I never go down the wrong path, I won't make trouble for myself. And Jesus can help us stay with him today, tomorrow, and every day. Then we can outsmart the fox and live with God forever."

LIFE APPLICATION PAGE

For Small Group Leaders
• WEEK EIGHT •

- **Promise Path Action Topic:** Stay on the Promise Path
- **Desired Outcome:** That kids will identify one thing to work on that will help them stay on the Promise Path.
- **Bible Story:** Matthew 28:1–10
- **Promise Path Memory Verse:** You will teach me God's way to live. Being with you will fill me with joy. At your right hand I will find pleasure forever. Psalm 16:11 (ICB) (older children); You will teach me God's way to live. Psalm 16:11 (ICB) (younger children)

THINGS YOU'LL NEED

- Copy of "Tips for Small Group Leaders" (p. 21)
- *Bug Beepers for Promise Keepers* Critter County Activity Book (K–2)
- *Promise Kids on the Promise Path* Children's Journal (3–6)
- Promise Kids Prayer Poster
- Promise Path Action Topic Poster
- Newsprint and/or copy paper
- Markers
- Chalkboard and chalk
- Construction paper
- Large outline patterns of a church (one per student)
- Scissors
- Stapler

KID TALK

Today is the last day with your Small Group. You may wish to decorate the room for a small party to celebrate the Resurrection. The Promise Path Action Topic is Stay on the Promise Path. This is an excellent opportunity for reviewing all the action topics—all the ways to follow God's directions. Begin your review using these questions:
• **Why is it important for us to stay on the Promise Path?**
• **Let's review our Promise Path Action Topics. These topics will help us get started when it comes to staying on the Promise Path.** Review each topic with your group. As the topics are named, ask kids to briefly describe one way they could follow through on them after the Adventure.
• **Name some ways you can stop and think about Jesus.**

• **How can you find friends who will help you follow Jesus?**
• **What are some things you can do that Jesus would do?**
• **How can you make family time important?**
• **How can you get involved at church?**
• **How can you accept others as Jesus does?**
• **How can you make a difference in the world?**
  Encourage children to choose one idea from the discussion to focus on in the coming week.

GROUP-BUILDING ACTIVITY
(You may want to do this activity earlier in the session.)

  If time permits, do the following group-building activity. Distribute the above supplies and ask everyone to make their own Promise Path Church Book. Copy the church pattern on construction paper and cut it out for the covers of their books. Then cut several sheets of newsprint or copy paper for the inside pages—these can be church-shaped or square.
  Instruct children to staple the cover and pages together on one side, title the book "Promise Kids on the Promise Path," and decorate as desired.
  On the inside of the book, ask kids to write down the Promise Path Action Topics. Then use the rest of the pages for autographs of the children in the Small Group. Tell kids to write something they appreciate about the owner of the book. They can then use this as a reminder of the Promise Path experience and Promise Kids met during the Adventure.

PRAYER TALK

Let's celebrate being Promise Kids by saying our Promise Kids Prayer one more time together. Then we'll thank God for our Adventure and ask him to help us stay on the Promise Path!
  Using the Promise Kids Prayer Poster, read the

prayer together with your group. Encourage kids to finish the prayer, if they feel comfortable, by telling God one way they will stay on the Promise Path.

SMALL GROUP TIP

As your 50-Day Adventure draws to a close, help kids to see each day as a new opportunity to stay on the Promise Path. Remind them to yield, by slowing down to think about how their actions and words will affect others, and whether or not their actions are a reflection of their desire to follow God's directions. Remind kids that they have learned very important habits they will want to keep for a lifetime, and that by doing so, they will stay on the Promise Path one day at a time.

For a dynamic, hands-on learning experience that can help your students understand how to apply Bible stories to everyday life, try some of the following projects. This symbol 🕸 means that a project will require extra setup time or has special requirements (for example, kitchen use or an adult with woodworking experience).

WHAT ARE LIFE APPLICATION PROJECTS?

Life Application Projects are learning experiences that help participants apply the Bible-based Promise Path Action Topics to everyday life. Bible accounts become more than just stories as kids learn how to remember and apply them in the days ahead. Through meaningful crafts, games, or other activities, kids use the Promise Path Projects as a reminder of the action topics they learned and/or a practice tool for ongoing participation in them.

You can allot 20–45 minutes per activity, depending on your situation. (See the chart on p. 8 in the section "How Long Do I Spend on Each Part of the Session?") At each site, children are encouraged to work together to complete a project that demonstrates what they've learned. Because figuring out how to make the project is part of the learning experience, there are some projects that may not have step-by-step instructions. This will provide the children a richer learning experience and more ownership of what they create. The adult or older teen leaders working in the Life Application Project areas should guide, rather than direct, the activities. The leaders also can help the children understand how each project relates to the Promise Path Action Topics.

HOW DO THE LIFE APPLICATION PROJECTS WORK?

• Life Application Project work sites should be set up to accommodate 10 to 12 kids each, with one leader for each site.
• During each session, kids choose their own project sites and decide how long they will work at each one. (A child may choose to spend 10 minutes at one project area and then join a different project.) Some kids may choose to work at the same site for all eight weeks, whereas others may opt to rotate to a number of different sites from week to week. Some of the projects offered in this section can be done in one or two weeks' time, while others may take the full eight weeks to complete. That information is noted in the project instructions. Kids in grades K–6 will intermingle with one another, each contributing to the projects according to his or her development level.

• It is the site leader's responsibility to provide his or her site with suitable supplies and directions for completing the project. As kids arrive, they must read the directions to figure out how to use the supplies in completing the project.
• New project sites can be added as the children complete or lose interest in old ones. Some project sites will be more appropriate to certain sessions than others. Certain projects require consistency among workers if the aim is a group presentation of some sort.
• On the first day of the Adventure, the children should be given a quick look at each of the projects and allowed to choose the one they want to work on first.
• If you have chosen to run the Adventure in a more traditional church school setting—one teacher, one class, one room—just pick a couple of projects appropriate for your group to do each week. (If possible, offer more than one so kids have a choice.)

HOW MUCH WORK IS THIS GOING TO BE?

It is important to note that you have control over how complicated or simple you want to make each of the Life Application Projects and how elaborately you will furnish the area. The suggested projects are just that—suggestions. Feel free to simplify, replace, or develop projects with ideas of your own.

The hardest part of the Life Application Projects is done before the Adventure begins. Once you have selected the projects and gathered the resources, the majority of your time will be spent overseeing the setup from week to week. Don't be shy about asking people for help when you need it. The most successful programs are usually the result of team efforts rather than solo performances.

HOW DO I GET ORGANIZED?

Start with a brainstorming and planning session with all of your leaders and adult or older teen helpers to decide which projects will work best for your group. Have this meeting six to eight weeks before the Adventure begins. Try answering questions such as:

• How many projects will we need? (A good rule of thumb is one project for every 10 to 12 kids.)

• Which projects will our kids enjoy the most?

• How much space is available for project sites?

• What are the strongest interests and talents among our project leaders?

• What project resources are readily available?

• What projects will work best within the budget?

• How will we set up and decorate each project site area?

• How can the projects be stored?

If you offer projects that involve working with nails, needles, kitchen equipment, and other activities that require extra care, you would be wise to have parents sign a permission slip. See page 22.

WHERE CAN I FIND SUPPLIES FOR THE PROJECTS?

You will need to obtain the supplies necessary to complete each of your projects. After a thorough search of your own supply room, think about borrowing items from church members and other local churches. You can publicize your needs via a church bulletin, newsletter, bulletin board, or by sending a letter home to parents or all members of the congregation. If you still come up short on project supplies, try these places:

• Craft store
• Hardware store
• Christian bookstore
• Art supply store
• School supply store

Be careful to include all supplies needed to accomplish your goal. Give thought to measuring, cutting, gluing, writing tools, and work-area protection before you begin.

WHAT DO I NEED TO KNOW ABOUT SETTING UP THE PROJECT SITES?

Exercise care and caution when assigning site areas for each project. Give consideration to:

• The amount of space needed to complete the project.

• The noise level involved in construction or rehearsal of a project.

• The mess factor involved in the project. (Projects requiring water, hand washing, or other special needs should be located near water-access areas.)

Project sites can be flexible according to your church's available space. If you have one large room, you can use it for both the Life Application Projects and the Bible Story Presentation. Put each project on tables that can be moved around as needed. Projects too large for tables could be done on the floor. If you have several smaller classrooms, you could put one or two projects in each room. Just make sure the kids know where all the projects are so they can find them easily. Projects can even be worked on in a hallway (on tables) as long as people meeting in nearby rooms can close the doors to keep out the chatter of enthusiastic workers! Decorating the project sites is optional. You may wish to design canopies over them or design them as different rooms of the Promise Path Factory. Decorate however you wish to fit in the project theme.

WHO DOES THE CLEANUP?

Allow for several minutes at the end of each project time to clean up. The project leader should give direction as to what is expected. Kids may collect supplies, pick up scraps, and clean the area.

If your timeframe is tight and an extra five minutes can't be found for cleanup, the children could do a minimal straightening and the adult at the project site could put things away while the kids are at Bible Story Time or when they leave to go home.

WHERE DO I STORE THE PROJECTS?

How you store the projects will depend on their type and size. Paper projects might be rolled up, stacked, kept in a file folder, or placed in a box. Small, three-dimensional projects might be kept in boxes or bins on a cabinet shelf. Large projects might be placed on top of a storage cabinet or locked in a storage room. You may wish to obtain one or two carts with wheels that can hold several bins as well as stackable items. Roll the carts into your project area at the start of each day, and roll them back into storage when you are done. Label each project for easy reference, and include a sign that reads, "Please don't touch! This is a 50-Day Adventure project!"

HOW CAN I HELP PROJECTS SUCCEED?

• The best learning experiences happen when participants take part in, discover, think, handle, and question. Leaders need to encourage the kids to experiment, create, and seek their own answers at every stage of a project.

• Leaders need to be sure kids understand how the projects relate to everyday life or the 50-Day Adventure. Leaders can do this by encouraging the children to answer simple questions provided with each project, and to discuss their impressions and opinions as they work.

• Each child will have his or her own personal abilities. Leaders should provide as much help as the children need—but no more. Rather than "teach," leaders should encourage children to discover and experience. Leaders need to help children discover where their strengths lie.

• To be sure all the leaders understand the big picture of Promise Kids on the Promise Path and grasp how Life Application Projects fit in, give each leader a copy of "The Big Picture" (pp. 5–8), "Ready to Begin: Weekly Leader Information" (pp. 13–20), and this section.

• Have the projects set up and ready to begin about 20 minutes before the start of class. As soon as the children arrive they can begin to work. This option works even if you choose to offer the Life Application Projects as the last portion of your session.

• The first week or two, the kids will need plenty of guidance to understand this new approach. The leaders need to keep reinforcing the idea that the kids can try any project they like and even switch projects if they choose.

• It's helpful to have basic instruction posters taped to the table or wall at each project area. That way kids can take more initiative for figuring out what to do. In particular, provide written directions for projects that involve measuring, mixing, researching, and building.

THE PROJECTS

You can use the following suggestions or think of your own creative ideas. Be sure to have adult or older teen supervision at each project site. Also, it may be wise to make a sample of the more complex projects before tackling them with the children. This will enable you to discover the best way to help kids with the projects. But because you want the kids to use their own creativity, please refrain from showing your samples until the children have finished their projects (unless the project seems complex).

These projects are organized by age range with the easiest ones first. With help, the younger children can be successful in doing most of these projects.

1. PROMISE PATH PARADE

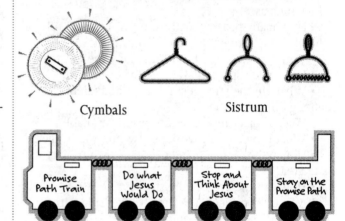

Cymbals   Sistrum

Promise Path Train | Do what Jesus Would Do | Stop and Think About Jesus | Stay on the Promise Path

Goal: Participants will put together a Promise Path Parade for presentation during Week 8. This will be done to celebrate the 50-Day Adventure as well as the resurrection of Jesus Christ.

Length: This project will take two to four weeks to complete and is suitable for all ages. It requires minimal preparation but will need extra storage space.

Supplies: See below.

Directions: Allow kids to be creative in thinking of ways to march and advertise what has been learned. They can make posters, flags, musical instruments, banners, vehicles (like the Promise Path Plane on p. 101—you might also add others like a train or bus), and floats. Here are several possibilities:

• **Musical Instruments:** You can make drums, tambourines, cymbals, horns, or other instruments. Encourage kids to use their imagination to come up with new ideas.

Sistrum: You will need wire hangers, wire cutters, fine-gauge wire, pliers, a yardstick, scissors, glue, tape, large buttons, and colorful strips of fabric.

Cut off the bottom of a wire hanger. Then bend the hooked end of a hanger into a loop and twist it closed with pliers. Bend each end of the hanger into a small closed loop and pull the ends together until approximately 10" wide. Next, cut a 15" piece of wire and attach it at one end of the hanger. Twist it around the closed loop, securing in place with pliers. Then thread about ten large buttons onto the wire and pull it tightly toward the opposite end of the hanger. Twist it around the closed loop and secure in place with pliers. Complete by wrapping strips of colorful fabric around the looped end of the hanger, gluing it in place to create a handle. Tape the end if needed. Shake the sistrum to a beat, just like a tambourine.

Cymbals: You will need aluminum pie tins, paper fasteners, felt, permanent markers, glue, and scissors.

Begin by cutting two 1" x 5" pieces of felt. Attach paper fasteners to each end of both felt strips, then punch them through the outside of the pie tins to hold in place. This will make a handle. Use colored permanent markers to decorate as desired. Hit them together in time to a beat.

• **Promise Path Train:** You will need several large cardboard boxes big enough for kids to stand inside, scissors or a utility knife, spray paint, paint and brushes, and 10" strips of metal chains.

Begin by cutting out the tops and bottoms of the boxes. You may need an adult to do the cutting work. Then create whatever shape you wish for your train by penciling it on the side of the box. Be sure that both sides match. Keep your shape simple so that it will be easier to cut. Consider an engine, box cars, and a caboose. Cut out the shapes, as well as a 2" x 5" hole one inch from the top of each upper center side of the cars to use as handles. Cut a small hole in the front and back of each box to attach a chain that will connect the cars. Spray paint each car a desired color. Then paint titles of the Promise Path Action Topics along the sides of the train to proclaim what has been learned during the Adventure. Let the paint dry. Attach the chains.

• **Float:** Create floats out of wagons that can be pulled. Give kids supplies like cardboard, construction paper, poster board, tissue paper, crepe paper, markers, scissors, glue, tape, sequins, ribbon, yarn, and other materials you have on hand. Let them create designs of their choice, but encourage them to proclaim a Promise Path Action Topic in their decorating. Pull the wagon as a parade float.

Questions: As the children work, ask these questions or ones similar to them: **Why do we have parades? How can we present our Promise Path Parade to show what we've learned during our 50-Day Adventure? Why should we celebrate Jesus' resurrection? What did Jesus do for us when he died on the cross, then rose from the dead?**

 Kindergarten Suggestion: Encourage the younger children to help with the float or make the cymbals, since these projects involve no difficult cutting.

2. PROMISE PATH PHOTO ALBUM

Goal: Participants will make a Promise Path Photo Album as a reminder of their 50-Day Adventure.

Length: This project can be worked on every week of the Adventure and it is suitable for all ages. It requires minimal preparation and storage, but it may require additional supplies and cost.

Supplies: Camera (instant or flash), photo album (which can be purchased or made), tape or glue, pens, and costumes and props for pictures

Directions: Kids will take pictures of scenes recreated from the weekly Bible story as well as pictures of ways to apply them to everyday life.

• Begin by asking the children to review the week's Promise Path Action Topic and story.

• Have them decide on three or four ways to recreate the Bible story in a scene(s). Use costumes, simple backdrops, and easy-to-find props, if necessary. Take pictures.

• Next, think of ways to apply the Bible story and Promise Path Action Topic to everyday life. Once again, select two or three ways, then create scenes for pictures. Take the pictures.

• If you have an instant camera, you can immediately put the pictures into the photo album. Take time to label each picture with an appropriate caption.

• If you need to get the photos developed, have each group add the pictures that were taken the previous week to the photo album. Caption them accordingly.

Questions: Ask these questions, or similar ones, as the children work: **When did you first learn about God? When did you realize the importance of following God's directions? What are some of the ways you already follow his directions? What are some of the ways you can better follow his directions?**

3. PROMISE PATH LAMPS OR CANDLES

Goal: The children will make lampshades or candle holders that will proclaim the Bible verse "You should be a light," taught in Week 7.

Length: This project will take one week and is suitable for all ages.

Supplies: *Lampshade*—old smooth-sided lampshades, ruler, large maps, ribbon, glue, string, hole punch, plastic sewing needle, scissors, and a permanent marker

Candleholder—baby-food jar, scissors, glue, different-colored tissue paper, permanent marker, paper cup, paintbrush, pencil with eraser, small votive candles, matches or lighter (if desired)

Directions for Lampshade:
• Measure the height and top circumference of the shade you will be using. Add 1" to the height and multiply the top measure by three.
• Cut a rectangle matching the above measurements out of a large map. Use additional maps if needed, and glue them together. Write the words "You Should Be a Light" in large letters across the center of the map.
• Use a ruler to draw light lines one inch apart along the entire length of the map. Fold, accordion style, along each marked line. Make certain that each line is firmly creased.
• Bring the two ends of the map together to create a tube. Glue them together.
• Use a paper punch to puncture holes in the center of each pleat along the top edge of the map. The holes should be approximately 1/4" from the top. Then thread a ribbon through the holes, using a plastic needle.
• Spread glue over the top 1/2" of the shade. Slip the map over the shade and pull the ribbon so that the pleats fit along the rim. Knot the ribbon and tie a bow or cut off the remaining strands. Work with the pleats so that they are evenly spread around the circumference of the shade. Let dry.
• Spread 1/2" of glue along the bottom of the shade. Then tie string around the pleated map along the bottom and knot. Once again, work with the pleats so that they are evenly spread around the bottom circumference of the shade. Let dry, then cut and remove the string.
• Place the shade on a lamp. When the light is turned on, it will proclaim "You Should Be a Light" for all to see!

Directions for Candleholder:
• Cut different colors of tissue paper into 1/2" squares.
• Pour glue into a paper cup or small container and add a few drops of water until the glue becomes thin.
• Use a paintbrush to spread the glue onto the baby-food jar, working with a third of the jar at a time.
• Using the eraser end of a pencil, pick up a square of tissue paper and place it on the glued area of the jar. Continue until the entire area has been covered. Repeat until the jar is covered with colored tissue paper. Then put on a second layer. Let dry.
• Using a permanent marker, write the words "You Should Be a Light!" across the jar.
• Insert a small votive candle, if desired. Caution children to light the candle only in the presence of an adult.

Questions: As the children work, ask questions similar to these: **What do you mean by "your light"?** (Explain that "our light" is the things we do that show we follow God's directions and love others.) **How can we let our lights shine out to others? How did Jesus' light shine in the world? How does that make a difference in the lives of everyone who believes in Jesus as their Savior?**

 Kindergarten Suggestion: Kindergartners are capable of making the candleholder. The leader will need to write the words on the jar. *Stop and think about Jesus.*
Find friends who help you follow Jesus.

4. PROMISE PATH KEY CHAINS
Do what Jesus would do.

Goal: Participants will make key rings that hold reminders of Promise Path Action Topics, Promise Path Memory Verses, or ways to follow God's directions by doing what Jesus would do. This project correlates with Week 3 as well as reviews each topic.

Length: This project will take one week to complete and is suitable for all ages. It requires minimal preparation, cleanup, and storage.

Supplies: Key rings, paper, clear contact paper, hole punch, markers, scissors, pencils, Bibles

Directions: Review the Promise Path Action Topics that have been discussed. Talk about ways to follow through on doing what Jesus would do. What Bible verses help to remind them of doing what Jesus would do?
• Have kids select a Christian symbol or shape to cut out of paper. Some suggestions include a fish, cross, heart, and star.
• Next, select a Promise Path Action Topic, Promise Path Memory Verse, or things Jesus would do that will help remind them to follow God's directions (for example: "I will love others," or "I will be helpful at home"). Write each one on a shape.
• Cover both sides of the shape with clear contact paper and trim the edges. Punch a hole in the shape and thread it onto the key ring. Carry the key chain as a reminder of the 50-Day Adventure.

Questions: Ask these questions or similar ones as the children work: **What are some ways we can do what Jesus would do? Keys open doors or locks. How are our Promise Path Action Topics keys to following God's directions? Is it always easy to do what Jesus would do? Why or why not? Why**

should we do what Jesus would do even when it's hard?

Kindergarten Supplies: Cardboard patterns of Christian Symbols.

Kindergarten Suggestion: Have the little ones trace the symbol onto paper. Because of the children's limited writing skills, the leader may need to write the topics or verses on the symbol.

5. PROMISE PATH FAMILY COUPONS

Goal: Participants will design a coupon book with family-time ideas inside it. This project correlates with Week 4.

Length: This project will take one week to complete and is suitable for all ages. It requires minimal preparation, cleanup, and storage.

Supplies: Card stock (8 1/2" x 11"), copy paper, ruler, scissors, pencils, stapler, markers, stickers, or other decorating supplies

Directions:

• Begin by folding the card stock in the center to make an 8 1/2" x 5 1/2" coupon holder. Staple the sides. Title it and decorate as desired.

• Brainstorm family-time ideas with the rest of the group. List them on a board so that everyone can share them.

• Cut copy paper into 5" x 8" sheets to make the coupons. Design coupons that give family members ideas of different ways to make family time important. For example: *This coupon is good for one outing at the zoo.* Decorate with animals. Take out of the coupon holder when your family is ready to put the activity on the calendar. Here are other ideas to get you started:

* Visits to a museum, park, aquarium, nature center, lake, forest preserve, or farm; outing on a train, boat, or to a movie; activities such as roller skating, ice skating, swimming, hiking, bowling, or camping; eating breakfast, lunch, or dinner out

* Service projects such as doing a walk-a-thon, helping with a food drive, going on a food scavenger hunt, helping at a homeless shelter, visiting the sick or shut-ins, singing Christmas carols at a nursing home, baking food to take to new neighbors, volunteering time at a local hospital, and cleaning up litter at a local school or park

* Time together at home doing chores, playing games, listening to music, playing charades, inviting friends and/or neighbors over, planning a backwards dinner, planning an indoor picnic, hosting an ethnic dinner, looking at photo albums, watching family videos, renting a movie and popping popcorn, telling stories, having a water gun or water balloon battle, and sharing information about favorite books.

Questions: As the children work, ask questions similar to these: **Why is it important to spend time with your family? How can family members be important in helping each other keep promises and follow God's directions?**

6. PROMISE PATH CHURCH CALENDAR

Goal: The children will make a year-long calendar to remind them of the Promise Path Action Topics. They can use it to chart their goals and participation in getting involved at church. This project correlates with Week 5 and helps review the entire Adventure.

Length: This project will take approximately one to two weeks to complete. It requires minimal preparation, cleanup, and storage and is suitable for all ages.

Supplies: 8 1/2" x 14" construction paper or card stock, wallpaper scraps or wrapping paper, scissors, glue, markers, pencils, hole punch, 12 photocopies of calendar grid (p.104) per child.

Directions:
• Fold 13 sheets of construction paper or card stock in half. Staple twice on the fold. Punch a hole through the top center of each of the 13 sheets for hanging the calendar. Reinforce by placing a small piece of clear tape over the portion of the sheet between the hole and the outer edge.

• Title the calendar "Promise Path Church Calendar" and decorate the cover as desired.

• Provide each participant with 12 photocopies of the monthly grid to glue onto the bottom part of each page. Label each grid with the appropriate month.

• Create a border around the top of each calendar page by using wallpaper scraps or wrapping paper. Inside the border, write one Promise Path Action Topic for each of eight months. Then challenge kids to come up with four additional action topics of their own to complete the calendar. Under each topic, children can write down ways to put that topic into practice.

• Tell kids to use the calendar to write down church events, worship times, and other gathering opportunities.

At the end of the calendar, kids can write themselves questions to follow up on how they did. They can look back at the calendar and check for answers. For example:

How many times did I go to Sunday school this year?

How many fellowship gatherings did I attend with my family?

How many times did I help out at church?

How many special worship services did I go to?

How many worship services did I participate in by doing something special (ushering, acolyting, reading, greeting, and so on)?

Questions: As the children are working, ask questions such as these: **Why is it important to get involved at church? What are some of the activities our church offers members as a way to get them involved? How are you involved at church right now? How do you plan to get involved at church in the future?**

 Kindergarten Supplies: Pictures of Jesus, church activities, children participating in church activities, church buildings, Sunday school classes, and so on. (These can be cut from magazines or old Sunday school leaflets. You can also copy simple pictures and let kids color them.)

Kindergarten Suggestion: Young children can glue a picture at the top of each page. The leader will need to help with writing the months.

7. PROMISE PATH T-SHIRTS

Goal: Participants will make a T-shirt with one of the Promise Path Action Topics printed on the front.

Length: One week—suitable for all ages.

Supplies: White T-shirts in various sizes (or you can ask kids to bring their own), fabric paint, paper, pencils

Directions: If you can't afford to purchase T-shirts for the children, send a note home telling parents about this Promise Path Project option and the week(s) it will be offered. Many parents will gladly send a T-shirt for their child to decorate.

• Have kids select a Promise Path Action Topic to put on their T-shirt. Have them draw some sample designs on paper.

• Lay the T-shirt out on a flat surface. Use pencils to lightly write the Promise Path Action Topic onto the shirt and sketch a picture or design to accompany it. Possible pictures might be a path, a handprint, a church, and so on.

• Use fabric paint to cover the pencil markings. Tell kids to exercise caution when using the paint, particularly when filling in large spaces. Too much paint will weigh the shirt down, and it won't be as comfortable to wear.

Questions: As the children work, ask questions like these: **Why did you choose this Promise Path Topic to put on your T-shirt? How are you going to live it out? Why is it important to follow God's directions?**

 Kindergarten Suggestion: Have the younger children use fabric markers instead of paint. They are easier to control.

8. FRIENDSHIP BRACELETS OR MEDALLIONS

Jim is a child of God

Goal: Participants will create a symbol of friendship that reminds them to find friends that will help them follow Jesus. Kids can create two symbols—one for themselves and one for a faithful friend. This correlates with Week 2.

Length: This project will take one to two weeks to complete and can be done by all ages—with help for the youngest children. It requires minimal preparation, cleanup, and storage.

Supplies: Bracelets will require letter beads and embroidery floss. Medallions will require air-drying clay, rolling pin, a glass, wooden stylus or pencil, and yarn. You may also use paint and brushes, if desired.

Directions: Try to do both symbols because the bracelet will probably be more appealing to the girls and the medallion to the boys.

• *Bracelet:* Select letter beads to spell out the name of a friend or the name "Jesus." Then cut six 12" lengths of embroidery floss in three different colors. Knot together at one end. Using the three different colors, begin braiding the floss, bringing each side over the center in alternating fashion for one-half to one inch. (This measurement will depend on the length of the name you chose and the size wrist you are working with!) Tie a knot, and string the first letter bead. Tie another knot, then repeat the process. If you have a long name, you may need to put two letters together at a time. After the last letter, measure it to the wrist and knot the ends together, allowing room for it to slip on and off.

• *Medallion:* Use a rolling pin to roll a golf ball-sized piece of clay to 1/4" thickness. Then turn a glass upside down and press it into the clay. Pull the excess clay out from around the glass and lift. Use a pencil to punch a hole in the top of the clay, taking care to leave 1/2" of clay between the hole and the outer edge.

Using a wooden stylus or pencil, create a saying or symbol, or write a friend's name. (For example: "Do What Jesus Would Do" or "Jimmy Is a Child of God.") Work the stylus slowly and carefully, removing the bits of clay that are etched out of the circle.

Let dry overnight.

When hard, lace a 20" piece of yarn through the hole and tie it. The medallion can be painted and covered with a glossy spray if desired.

• Instruct kids to give away their medallions or bracelets as one way to support friends who help them follow Jesus.

Questions: To help the children concentrate on why they are doing this project, ask questions like these. **How can friends help us to follow Jesus? Where can we find friends that will help us to follow Jesus? How can we be a friend to others and help them to follow Jesus? How can we invite new friends to follow Jesus?**

Kindergarten Suggestion: Have young children use yarn instead of embroidery floss to string the letters. They will need help spelling names and making knots. If they make medallions, have them print only "Jesus" on it. They will probably need help doing that.

9. PROMISE PACKAGES

Goal: Participants will make Promise Packages for new church members, newborn babies, or sick or shut-in members. This project correlates with Week 5, 6, or 7.

Length: Time is dependent upon the package being made. This project can be done by all ages—choose one easy option and one that is more challenging.

Supplies: Each option requires different supplies. (See below.)

Directions: There are a variety of Promise Packages kids can make. Offer at least two options. Select project recipients based on your church's needs. The following is an assortment of ideas to choose from:

• *For new members:* (Use caution and adult supervision when working with the oven.) Bake and decorate cookies or brownies. Use your favorite recipe, keeping in mind the length of time it takes to bake a product. Leaders may have to remove them from the oven after kids have already left. Or you may wish to prebake cookies and just have the kids decorate them. Place finished cookies on a small paper plate and keep them fresh by sliding the plate into a sealable baggie. Attach a card to accompany the package.

• *For sick or shut-ins:* Make paper maché vases with flowers. You will need an empty plastic bottle from a kitchen or bathroom product (and possibly a sharp knife for cutting it), flour, water, a bowl, a spoon, newspaper, paper towels, paint, brushes, white shoe polish, spray shellac, and scissors.

Begin by cutting the top off a plastic bottle, taking care to make it as even as possible. Adults should help children with this. Then mix 1 cup of flour with 3/4 cup of cold water and stir. A smooth paste will develop.

Next, tear newspaper into 1" x 6" strips. Dip them into the paste and wrap them over the outside of the bottle, covering it completely. Many strips will overlap. Be sure to cover the round lip of the vase where the lid was cut off. Repeat this process using white strips of paper towel instead of newspaper. Let dry until it is hard.

Paint with shoe polish and dry again.

Complete the vase by painting on a desired color or design. Spray it with shellac to finish.

Fill the vase with real flowers or create your own out of construction paper. Attach a card to accompany it.

• *For new births*: (Adult supervision is needed for the use of needles.) Cross-stitch bibs. You can obtain cross-stitch bibs at your local craft store. The bibs come with easy-to-stitch squares. Just add the pattern or lettering of your choice, lightly drawing it in with a pencil. You will need embroidery floss and plastic needles. Follow the diagram by sewing *Xes* over the pencil marks to create the picture or phrase of your choice. Attach a card to accompany it.

Questions: As the children work, ask questions like these: **Why is it important to get involved at church? What are some other ways to get involved at church besides offering gifts of kindness to others? How will our Promise Packages encourage others to get involved at church? How will our Promise Packages show others that we accept them as Jesus does?**

 Kindergarten Suggestion: Helping with the baking would be easiest for kindergartners. With assistance from the leader, they can make a vase or the flowers to go in it.

10. PROMISE PATH PRAYER BOOK

Goal: Participants will create a booklet to use when they stop to think about Jesus. This reinforces the lesson in Week 1.

Length: This project will take two to four weeks to complete and is most suitable for grades 2–6. It requires minimal preparation, cleanup, and storage.

Supplies: Construction paper, copy paper, lined paper, hole punch, ribbon, praying hands pattern, pencils, scissors, and markers.

Directions: Make copies of a pattern of praying hands, approximately 6" x 8" in size. You can find this in clip-art books and enlarge on a photocopy machine. Copy the pattern onto two sheets of construction paper and several sheets of copy and lined paper. Make as many sheets as you want in order to insert entries.

• Cut out each pattern.

• Punch two holes on the left-hand side of the pattern, making sure to punch holes in the same location on each pattern. Place the construction paper patterns on the top and bottom of the other patterns as a cover. Tie all of them together with ribbon.

• Title the booklet "Promise Path Prayer Book" and decorate as desired.

• Make entries on the inside pages using some of the following ideas:

* Copy favorite prayers.

* Make up prayers of your own, keeping in mind the eight Promise Path Action Topics for the Adventure.

* Draw pictures of things you are thankful for and want to remember as you stop to think about Jesus.

* Write poems about things that help you in thinking about Jesus.

* Write new words to familiar tunes to sing when you think about Jesus.

Questions: As children work on their booklet, ask questions like these: **Why should we stop and think about Jesus every day? What are some different ways to stop to think about Jesus? When you stop to think about Jesus, what comes to your mind? Why?**

Kindergarten Supplies: Same as above, eliminating scissors and ribbon and adding paper fasteners and stickers

Kindergarten Suggestion: Give the young children two construction paper patterns and two sheets of unlined paper patterns. Do not cut out the praying hands. Line up the pieces of paper with the construction paper for the covers, and punch two holes in the left side. Fasten together with paper fasteners. Help the children write the title on the cover. Decorate the cover with markers and stickers. Have the children draw things they are thankful for on one page and "Jesus" pictures on the other page.

II. PROMISE PATH ROAD SIGNS

Goal: Kids will make road signs that will help them remember the Promise Path Action Topics that follow God's directions.

🕐 **Length:** This project will take approximately two weeks to complete and is most suitable for children in grades 2–6. It can require minimal preparation and cleanup, depending on the type of signs you make.

Supplies: This project can be made in a variety of ways. You may construct signs out of *wood* (you will need precut wood, sandpaper, paint, and brushes); *burnt matchsticks* (you will need cardboard, heavy-duty scissors, preburnt matchsticks, and glue); *mosaic materials* (you will

Burnt matchsticks

MERGE

Embroidery

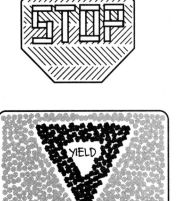

Mosaic materials

need cardboard or styrofoam meat trays, scissors, and any mosaic material such as aquarium gravel, various dry cereals, or different colored beans); *embroidery* (you will need styrofoam meat trays, yarn, and plastic needles); *paints* (you will need cardboard, scissors, paints, and brushes); or *markers* (you will need cardboard, markers, and heavy-duty scissors). Try to offer the kids two or three alternatives.

Directions: Before you start, review the names of the Promise Path Action Topics and the road signs used to introduce the topics. They are:

Stop and Think About Jesus—Stop sign
Find Friends Who Help You Follow Jesus—Pedestrian Crossing
Do What Jesus Would Do—Stoplight
Make Family Time Important—Construction Zone Ahead
Get Involved at Church—Merge
Accept Others as Jesus Does—Slippery Road Ahead
Make A Difference in the World—Walk
Stay on the Promise Path—Yield

• *For a wood sign:* Provide precut wood in various shapes. Smooth the wood by sanding it. Then select one of the topics and make a sign shape to match it. Use a pencil for words or symbols you want on the sign. Then paint over the pencil marks and let it dry. Cover with a glossy spray if desired.

• *For a burnt matchsticks sign:* Have kids cut the

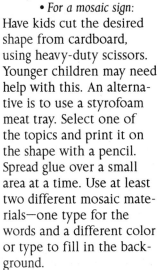

desired shape from cardboard, using heavy-duty scissors. Younger children may need help with this. Have them select one of the topics and print it on the shape with a pencil. Arrange matchsticks in creative ways to spell out the topic. Glue the matchsticks in place when the design is complete.

• *For a mosaic sign:* Have kids cut the desired shape from cardboard, using heavy-duty scissors. Younger children may need help with this. An alternative is to use a styrofoam meat tray. Select one of the topics and print it on the shape with a pencil. Spread glue over a small area at a time. Use at least two different mosaic materials—one type for the words and a different color or type to fill in the background.

• *For an embroidery sign:* (Adults need to supervise the use of the needles. Caution the children to take care when sewing.) Select a topic and pencil it onto cardboard or a styrofoam meat tray. You can also make some decorations or symbols. Then thread 20 inches of yarn through a plastic needle to stitch the lettering and/or symbols you have drawn. Thread the yarn onto a needle and tie a knot at the end of the yarn. Sew by poking the needle through the tray and turning the tray back and forth. When the yarn comes to an end, untie the needle and begin again, changing colors if you wish. You can use the yarn to outline the lettering and/or symbols, or you can use it to fill in the letters and/or symbols. The second idea will take a lot more time and yarn. Be careful when working with needles.

• *For a marker or paint sign:* Cut cardboard to a desired shape, using heavy-duty scissors. Younger children may need help. Select a topic and pencil in the sign that goes with it. Use paint or markers to trace the letters and decorate the sign.

Questions: As the children work, ask these questions to reinforce the Promise Path Action Topics: **How does this sign introduce what we are learning about? How does this sign relate to the Promise Path Action Topic? How do this sign and topic relate to you? How will you follow through with this activity? Where will you hang this sign as a reminder to stay on the Promise Path?**

Kindergarten Suggestion: Have the children select the sign shape and trace around the pattern for that shape. Print the words in block capital letters (this can be done by a leader or an older child). Have the children color in the letters with crayons or markers.

12. PROMISE PATH RESEARCH

Goal: Participants will research other cultures to help them explore ways to accept others as Jesus does and make a difference in the world. This project will also introduce kids to countries and customs they're not familiar with, helping kids to be more open to thinking about people beyond their direct experience. This project relates to Weeks 6 and 7.

Length: Varies. Children can work on the project for one week or several, depending on whether they research one country or many countries. This project is most suitable for older children (grades 3–6).

Supplies: Choose countries that your church works with in various mission opportunities, or select lands that you think would be interesting to young people. Provide a variety of research information such as mission organizations' materials, children's encyclopedias and books about other countries or cultures, and ethnic and cultural pictures, costumes, food, and music. Additional supplies are listed below.

Directions: Offer a different country each week, or change countries every two weeks. If you know someone from a different country, invite him or her to talk to the children and answer questions.

• Decorate your area by displaying the selected country's flag, props, costumes, and foods. Play music that is customarily heard in the country you will study.

• As kids enter your area, present them with a Promise Path Passport. On the passport, label the name of the country the child is "visiting" as well as the date and the child's name. If you have an instant camera, take a picture and attach it to the passport as a remembrance of the experience.

• Go to the library and obtain books that provide you with pictures, customs, foods, traditions, costumes, descriptions of important places, history, and events that kids can discover about the country. This is a great opportunity to use computers or CD ROMS if you have them available to you. Assist kids with research by asking questions that will help them in their search for information:

What are some of main foods in this country? Which ones would you like to try?

How do the people in this country dress? Are their clothes different from what you wear? How?

What important places are in this country? What historic events took place here? Have you heard of them before?

What are some of the customs and traditions of the people in this country? Which ones are the same and which ones are different from customs in your country?

Would you like to visit this country? Why or why not?

• If possible, let kids cook and taste some of the traditional foods of the country. This will help create a more memorable experience.

• For added fun, ask kids to use their research to write a descriptive paragraph, poem, or story about the people there. Display their writings on a bulletin board or in your church narthex.

Questions: Ask these questions to help the children clarify their ideas and connection to other countries and peoples: **How can you help make a difference in the world by reaching out to people in another country? How can you make a difference to people far away? How can you show your acceptance of people from other countries when they visit or live here?**

Kindergarten Supplies: Picture books of children in different countries or who come from other cultures, copies of simple pictures of children from countries around the world, markers or crayons

Kindergarten Suggestion: The little ones can "research" by looking at the picture books and coloring pictures of children from other countries.

13. TOPOGRAPHICAL PROMISE PATH

Goal: The children will design a neighborhood similar to their own to illustrate ways to stay on the Promise Path by following God's directions. This project correlates with Week 8.

 Length: This project will take approximately five to eight weeks to complete and is best suited for older children (grades 3–6). You may choose to have the entire group work on one large project or allow children to make their own miniature versions of a neighborhood.

Supplies: Some possible supplies are cardboard, wood, blocks, pea gravel, tiny artificial plants, sticks, cardboard, toothpicks, fabric, styrofoam, construc-

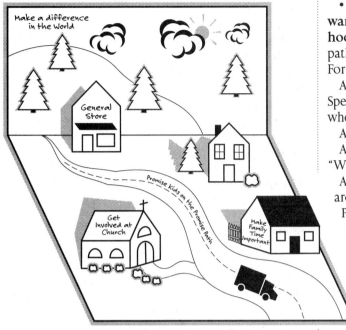

Make a difference in the World

General Store

Promise Kids on the Promise Path

Get Involved at Church

Make Family Time Important

• Ask **What kinds of places and paths do you want to include in your Promise Path neighborhood?** Encourage kids to think of creative areas or paths that lead toward following God's directions. For example:

A fork in the road with a sign that says: "Fast-track Speedway this way" or "Cloverleaf Meadow—a place where you can stop and spend time with Jesus"

A road called "Friendship Avenue"

A road called "Path of Wisdom" leading to "Wisdom Point"

A place called "Valley of Decisions" where there are a variety of questions correlating to the Promise Path Action Topics

Promise Path Potholes—road problems that kids have to solve leading to each week's Promise Path Action Topic

Temptation Turnpike—a place where kids are challenged with questions relating to what Jesus would do

Global Cafe—a place to meet many different people

Promise Path Church—a place to get involved with your church family where each door and window of the church opens up and offers a different way to participate

Promise Path detours—various turnoffs that lead to temptation

Promise Path street lamps that tell of ways to let your faith shine and make a difference in the world

Promise Path sports arenas or fields—places where kids can go to "Kick a goal for Jesus by . . ." or "Touch down here while you stop and think about Jesus by . . ." or "Free throw to get rid of temptations that lead you away from Jesus," and so on

Questions: As the children work on the project, ask questions such as these: **What are the Promise Path Action Topics? What choices can we make to help us follow God's directions? Why is it important to stay on the Promise Path wherever we go? What are some ways to stay on the Promise Path every day?**

Kindergarten Supplies: 24" x 18" poster board, construction paper, scissors, glue, and markers

Kindergarten Suggestion (this can also be used by all children to make the project simpler):

For little ones wanting to make their own neighborhood, consider doing a construction paper pop-up neighborhood.

Fold the top third of the poster board to create a

tion paper, sequins, air-drying clay, craft sticks, miniature cars and/or people, markers, paints, glue, tape, ruler, and scissors.

Directions: Numerous neighborhood models can be made by students wanting to work on this project. Children may create one model for the entire group, or work on individual projects of their own. Encourage creativity while telling students to keep the following in mind:

• Use a sturdy piece of cardboard or a piece of plywood as the base for the model.

• Think about the kinds of buildings and landscapes in your neighborhood. Is it a country setting with farm buildings and fields? Is it a busy city filled with skyscrapers, people, and cars? Is it a suburban area with houses, malls, and a downtown area?

• What type of materials would work best in building your neighborhood?

• How can you create Promise Path street signs that show people in the neighborhood the way to follow God's directions? Some examples might include:

"Slippery Road Ahead—don't let possible friends slip away from you!" Put it before a bridge that crosses a river.

"Construction Zone Ahead—family builders working at togetherness." Put it at a home construction site.

"Pedestrian Crossing—gather here to meet new friends that help you follow Jesus." Put it by a street leading to a church or school.

• Place a stoplight at intersections with different questions asking what Jesus would do in a particular situation.

backdrop for your scene. Glue or color a sky, hill, sun, clouds, and background trees on this part. Then color the bottom of the poster board with green grass and blue lakes or rivers. Color or glue on a winding path or road that leads through the ground and narrows toward the edge of the backdrop. This will give the illusion of the road continuing.

Create houses by cutting out several house shapes and gluing on paper windows, doors, and shutters. To make the scene three-dimensional, fold back the lower 1/2" of each house and glue it onto the bottom of the poster board. Add shrubs, flowers, trees, and picket fences around the houses, using the same method. Create several signs along the path with the ideas suggested above or by creating your own. Add miniature toy cars and people as desired.

14. PROMISE PATH FAMILY MAILBOX

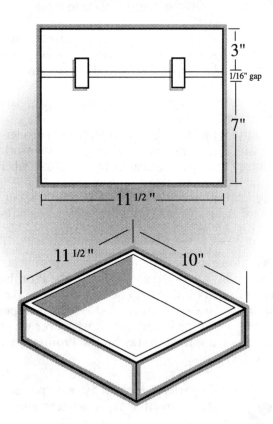

Goal: Participants will create an indoor mailbox for family members to use. The box will encourage family members to plan, communicate, surprise, and remember people in their family on a daily basis at home. This project correlates with Week 4.

Length: This project will take approximately three weeks and is most suitable for older chil-

dren (grades 3–6). It may require additional preparation and storage.

Supplies: Wood (pine board and plywood work well), sandpaper, nails, two 1 1/2" hinges with nuts and bolts, hammer, screwdriver, drill with 1/8" bit, wood stain, brush, paper, wood glue, family photo or drawing of the family, clear contact paper

Directions: (Careful adult supervision is needed for the use of hammers, screwdrivers, and drill. Talk to the children about tool safety before they begin.) If you have someone in your church that enjoys woodworking, ask him or her to help with this project.

Provide precut pieces of unfinished wood. (Often local hardware stores will offer churches a discount for wood projects or even scrap wood at little or no cost. Because of this, don't restrict yourself to finding any particular kind of wood, although pine board and plywood do work well. Most woods and widths will work unless they are very heavy or thick.) The following pieces are needed for each box:

one 10" x 11 1/2" quarter-inch plywood for bottom
one 3" x 11 1/2" quarter-inch plywood for lid
one 7" x 11 1/2" quarter-inch plywood for lid
four 10" x 3 1/2" x 1" pine board for sides
two 1 1/2"-long hinges
half-inch or slightly longer bolts and nuts that will fit hinge mounting holes

• Lightly sand all cut edges. Assemble sides with glue to make a 10" x 11 1/2" rectangle. Nail corners.
• Attach bottom using glue. Then nail.
• Glue small lid piece flush with top edge of box. Then nail.
• Fit larger lid piece over remaining opening in box. Leave a 1/16" gap between the two lid pieces. Position hinges over the 1/16" gap approximately two inches in from either side. Use a marker or pencil to mark the holes. (Some children may want to temporarily "attach" the lid by fastening it with masking tape during this step and for the drilling step below.)
• Remove hinges and drill holes. Use nuts and bolts to attach hinges.
• Take a family photo—or draw a family picture—cover with clear contact paper, and glue onto the lid.

Use the box as an indoor family mailbox to encourage family members to think about each other all year long. Family members can write each other letters, leave surprises, draw pictures, or just leave a note of encouragement. Check it daily!

Questions. As the children work, ask: **Why is it important to make time for your family? How can you make time for your family? What are**

some favorite things you like to do with your family? What are some things you plan to put into the family mailbox?

Kindergarten Supplies: Large cardboard shoebox, construction paper or wrapping paper, glue or tape, scissors, markers, decorative materials, 5" x 7" family photo or drawing of each child's family, clear contact paper

Kindergarten Suggestion (alternative for an easier project): Cover a shoebox and lid with wrapping paper or construction paper, wrapping the box and lid separately. Decorate the box using markers, glitter, ribbon, sequins, or other creative materials. Cover a 5" x 7" family photo or drawing of the family with contact paper, and glue it to the lid.

15. PROMISE PATH GAME

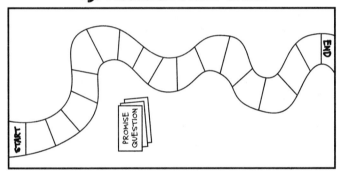

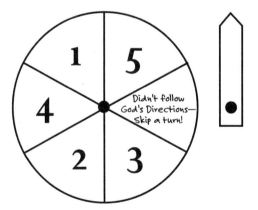

Goal: Children will create their own Promise Path game designed to encourage them to follow God's directions.

Length: This project will take approximately two weeks to make and one week to play and is most suitable for older children (grades 2–6). It requires minimal preparation, cleanup, and storage.

Supplies: Cardboard, card stock (manila file folders), unlined index cards, paper fasteners, game pieces, markers, scissors, construction paper, hole

punch

Directions:

• Use a large piece of cardboard or poster board to create a base for your game. Draw a twisting, winding path that goes all over a large part of the board. Make sure you have a beginning and an end. Using a permanent marker, draw 2" squares along the path.

• Create a spinner by cutting a 9" circle from card stock. Use a marker to divide the circle into six pie shapes. Cut a 4" x 1/2" arrow out of the card stock. Punch a small hole in the square end and attach it to the center of the circle with a paper fastener. Write the numbers 1–5 on five pie shapes. Put the phrase "Didn't follow God's directions—skip a turn" on the sixth piece.

• Use the index cards to make a deck of Promise Question Cards. On each card, write a challenging question relating to each week's Promise Path Action Topic. For example: "Name one thing you can do to stop and think about Jesus" or "Name one friend you know who will help you follow Jesus," and so on. Make at least eight cards.

• On many of the gameboard path squares, write a variety of ways to follow or not follow God's directions. Then decide if each of those ways deserves moving ahead or backward one, two, or three spaces. For example: *Invited a friend to church—move ahead two spaces;* or *Helped serve food at the homeless shelter—move ahead three spaces;* or *Forgot to stop and think about Jesus today—move back two spaces;* or *Forgot to say "I love you" to my parents this week—move back three spaces,* and so on.

• To play the game, kids will need a game piece. This can be a button, penny, or piece of colored paper. Use the spinner to determine how many spaces to move or if you lose a turn. After moving the correct number of spaces, follow the directions, if any, on the square. Then pick a Promise Question Card and answer the question before the next child has his or her turn. Place the card on the bottom of the pile. The first one to get through the Promise Path is the winner!

Kindergarten Suggestion (also recommended for beginning readers): Let the little ones color in background trees, rocks, and so forth, on the gameboard. When the game is played, pair younger and older children together to play as teams. That way the older children can read the cards and directions on the path. Kids can take turns moving the game piece.

BIBLE-TIME DRAMA

Children will prepare a drama based on Matthew 28:1–10, the resurrection of Jesus Christ. This will be presented as the Week 8 Bible Story Presentation. Students will be encouraged to put together this drama as an example of working together with friends who help them follow Jesus.

Length: This project will require the same participants each week so that they can plan, prepare, and practice for their performance on Week 8. The students will need to decide how extensive they want to get with set design, costumes, script writing, and memorization. This project will take at least five weeks to develop and is best for older children (grades 3–6).

Supplies: Bibles, Bible-time costumes for all characters, scenery, and props as noted in the suggestions that follow

Directions: Begin by reading Matthew 28:1–10 with the group. Let children suggest ways to act out the story. Remind kids that the Promise Path Action Topic for Week 8 is "Stay on the Promise Path." Read Matthew 27, the events leading up to the Resurrection, to give you some background on the scene.

Guidelines for Drama

1. Kids must settle on a drama style that everyone is comfortable with. Here are some questions to get children thinking about a style:

• Will the action take place exactly as told in the Bible?
• Will the story be told by "witnesses" to the action or by one of the women who was directly involved in it?
• Do you want to use the suggested script or write one of your own? If students plan to write their own, ask: Will it be an interview with the main characters in the story?
• Do you want to present a modern-day drama reflecting back on the Bible story?
• Do you want to act out the story or use puppets?

2. If students are writing their own script, they must decide which scenes will be necessary and what characters will be needed.

3. Here is a scripted suggestion for you to use:

BACKGROUND. The scene takes place north of Jerusalem. This is where Joseph of Arimathea buried Jesus' body after asking Pilate for permission. Joseph brought linen cloth to the cross, took the body down, wrapped it in the linen, and then placed it in a tomb cut out of rock. A large stone was rolled against the entrance of the tomb. Then the tomb was sealed and guarded by soldiers.

CHARACTERS. Luke 8:2 says that Jesus delivered *Mary Magdalene* from evil spirits. The other *Mary* was probably the wife of Clopas (the brother of Joseph). She may also have been the mother of James and the sister of Jesus' mother. This Mary was present at the crucifixion of Jesus.

The *guards* were soldiers stationed to watch over the burial place of Jesus. There is not a specific number of guards mentioned in this passage, but there were more than one. You may use any number of guards to allow more children to enter into the action of the story.

Jesus appears to the women and should be dressed in white (Luke 24:40). The *angel* also should be dressed in white.

If you have a large group of young people wanting to be involved in the drama, you might consider adding another scene, using the passage from Matthew 28:16–20 in which Jesus appears to the 11 disciples.

SCENERY. Outdoor scenery is needed. Create a backdrop of a big hill with a cave in it. Paint the inside of the cave black. Then cut a large stone out of cardboard and paint it gray. Use this to roll over the entrance to the tomb.

The tomb was probably built into the side of a large hill. It can be surrounded by plants, trees, and shrubs. Use artificial plants, bring in large planters, or create some plants out of sturdy cardboard. Since the tomb was carved out of a hill, a number of loose rocks can be strewn around the area.

COSTUMES. The women should wear long, plain tunics with scarves for their heads and sandals on their feet. Jesus and the angel should wear robes of white. The guards should wear short gray or brown tunics and hold shields and swords.

SCRIPT. The following script may be used, or you can revise it to fit your class:

(The two women are slowly walking toward the tomb as they are talking. They should look sad and upset.)

Mary M: I don't think I've ever seen a day as sad as the day they crucified Jesus.

Other Mary: I know what you mean. First they made Jesus carry his own cross all the way through Jerusalem and up the hill at Golgotha.

Mary M: And that happened after he was mocked in Pilate's court.

Other Mary: It had to be terribly humiliating.

Mary M: When the soldiers offered Jesus wine mixed with something to help kill the pain, he refused to drink it.

Other Mary: Jesus was very brave.

Mary M: Then they divided up his clothing by casting dice for it!

Other Mary: It was almost too much to bear. Above his head was that awful sign that sarcastically read, "This is Jesus, the King of the Jews."

Mary M: And the crowd yelled cruel things and made fun of Jesus.

Other Mary: "You said you were going to destroy the Temple and build it in three days. Save yourself!" they yelled.

Mary M: And they shouted to him to come down off the cross if he really was the Son of God.

Other Mary: But through all his suffering, Jesus forgave the people for what they were doing.

Mary M: When Jesus died, the ground shook.

Other Mary: I was so frightened! I was certain that it was God wanting to swallow us up for killing his Son!

Mary M: I even heard one of the guards shout that he believed Jesus was the Son of God after that happened.

Other Mary: I'm glad we are going to the place where Jesus was buried. I just need to be near to him right now.

Mary M: So do I.

(Women move to the side. Soldiers are sitting, half-asleep, around the tomb. Create a loud thundering sound by playing thunder on a sound effect cassette or by rattling a plastic wading pool. During the sounds, the guards should look frightened and pretend to be losing their balance. It should last for about 30 seconds.)

Guard 1: The ground is shaking under us!

Guard 2: What should we do?

Guard 1: I don't know! We can't leave the tomb or we'll be in terrible trouble.

Guard 2: But if we stay, I'm frightened that we'll die here!

(As the loud sound comes to an end, the angel rolls away the stone and sits on it. The guards fall to the ground as if they are dead. The women appear at the scene.)

Mary M: What's happening?

Other Mary: I don't know! It sounds like God is still angry!

Mary M: *(Pointing to the angel)* Mary, look! Let's get out of here.

Other Mary: Okay, hurry, let's go!

Angel: Don't be afraid! I know that you are looking for Jesus who was killed on the cross. But he is not here. He has risen from death, just as he said he would. Come and see the place where his body was.

Mary M: It's an angel of the Lord!

Other Mary: Do you think it could be true? Is Jesus really risen?

Mary M: We came all this way. Let's look inside the tomb and see if what the angel said is true.

(The women slowly and nervously walk to the tomb and look inside.)

Other Mary: Mary! It's empty!

Mary M: Do you think Jesus really has risen?

Angel: Run quickly and tell his disciples that Jesus has risen from the dead and will be going ahead of you to Galilee. There you will see him, just as I have told you. *(The angel leaves.)*

Mary M: This is wonderful news!

Other Mary: Let's go quickly and tell the others!

Mary M: Yes, we must! *(They cross to the other side of* *the stage where Jesus appears to them.)*

Jesus: Greetings!

(The women come close to Jesus and kneel down at his feet.)

Mary M: Jesus, is it really you?

Other Mary: We were told that you had risen, but it almost seemed too good to be true!

Jesus: Don't be afraid. Go and tell my disciples to go to Galilee, and there they will see me too.

Mary M: O Jesus, we will do just as you say! *(The women stand up as Jesus leaves.)*

Mary M: Mary, Jesus is risen!

Other Mary: He is risen indeed!

Mary M: Let's hurry and tell the others! *(The women hurry off stage.)*

Questions: To help kids understand the drama they are performing, ask questions like these: **How do you think the women felt when the earth shook and the angel rolled the stone away? How do you think the women felt when the angel appeared to them? When Jesus appeared to them?**

If Jesus appeared to you and gave you a job to do, what would you say? Jesus wanted everyone who witnessed his resurrection to go and spread the Good News. How can we continue to spread the Good News today? How can staying on the Promise Path help us to spread the Good News of Jesus?

Kindergarten Suggestion (also recommended for grades 1–2): Have the younger children be the soldiers. Tell them ahead of time what they are to do. Cue them when it is their turn to "act."

17. PROMISE PATH GAME SHOW

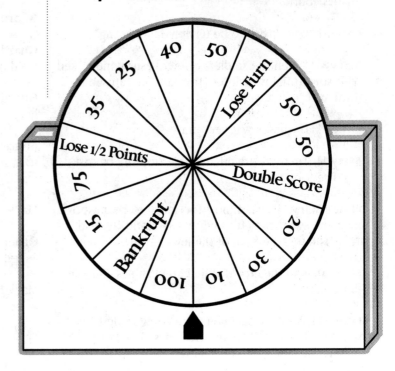

M _ K _ _ D I _ _ _ _ R _ N C _

I N   T H _   W O R _ D

Goal: Participants will create their own game show, "The Wheel of Promise," for reviewing the 50-Day Adventure.

Length: This project will take approximately three weeks to make and one week to play. This project is most suitable for the older children (grades 3–6). It requires extra preparation and storage.

Supplies: Thin cardboard, cardboard box, paint, markers, scissors or utility knife, paper, pencils, extra long paper fastener, list of Promise Path Action Topics and Promise Path Memory Verses, chalkboard and chalk or pad of newsprint

Directions:

• Begin by creating a 15" cardboard circle. Paint it, then segment it off into 16 equal pie pieces. On each pie piece, write one of the following: 5 points, 10 points, 15 points, 20 points, 25 points, 30 points, 35 points, 40 points, 45 points, 50 points, 75 points, 100 points, lose turn, bankrupt, double score, lose half your points.

• Paint a cardboard box a different color from your wheel. Punch a 1/4" hole one inch from the bottom center of one side of the box and turn it upside down. Punch another hole in the center of your wheel. Attach the wheel to the bottom of the upside-down box with an extra-long paper fastener so it will spin. If your cardboard is too thick for a paper fastener, use a long nut with a bolt. Twist the bolt in as far as you can while still allowing freedom of movement for the wheel. Paint a black arrow on the box below and pointing toward the wheel.

• To play, ask a leader to pick one of the Promise Path Action Topics or Promise Path Memory Verses. Then, on the chalkboard, create a series of blanks for each letter of each word in the topic or verse. Separate each word with an extra space. The first player begins by guessing a letter in the topic or verse and spinning the wheel. If the wheel lands on any of the point spaces, that child can earn the specified amount of points if the letter guessed comes up in the topic or verse. If the wheel lands on "Bankrupt," the player loses all points up to that time of play, as well as his or her turn. For "Lose Turn," the player skips one turn. For "Lose Half Your Points," the player loses half of his or her points (if any) and skips a turn. For "Double Points," the player doubles his or her points (recorded on the board) if a correct letter guess is made. If no points are on the board, the player spins the wheel until a point amount is reached and doubles that amount. If a player makes an incorrect letter guess, no points are earned. If a correct letter guess is given, the leader fills in all blanks for that letter on the board.

• Play continues to the next person, repeating the above directions. A player may make one guess at the topic or verse per turn. An exact match must be made to win the round. The correct guess adds 50 points to the score. The winner is the person with the most points.

Continue to play by selecting another leader who chooses a new topic or memory verse.

Questions: Where do we find God's directions? How do we know if our decisions are following God's directions? How can being a Promise Kid help you to follow God's directions? Why is it important to remember the Promise Path Action Topics?

 Kindergarten Suggestion (also first graders): Pair kindergartners with fifth or sixth graders to do this project.

18. PROMISE PATH PLANES

Make a Difference in the World!

Goal: To make airplanes large enough for kids to get inside. They will proclaim "Make a Difference in the World!" Planes can be used during the Promise Path Parade, which can be found on page 86. This project correlates with the lesson in Week 7.

Length: This project will take two or three weeks to complete and is best suited to older children (grades 3–6). It requires additional preparation and storage.

Supplies: Large cardboard boxes (big enough for one person to stand inside), scissors or utility knife, aluminum foil, masking tape, clear contact paper, spray paint, pencil, yardstick, extra cardboard, ribbon, large paper fastener, paints, and paint brushes

Directions:
• Remove the bottom of the box. Cut off each flap with scissors or a utility knife. (Adult supervision is needed for this step.)

• Cut wings approximately 15" long out of each side of the box. Shape as desired. Be sure that each wing is directly across from the other. Leave the top of each wing attached to the box, and make the wings high enough for children to slip their arms under. The kids will use these holes to stick their arms out and help hold the plane up when "flying."

• Next, cut a 10" x 10" square in the top of the box, for the children's head. Adjust size as necessary. You want the box to rest on each child's shoulders while he or she is inside the plane. Make sure the hole isn't large enough to slip over the children's shoulders.

• Cut two 15" x 5" strips of cardboard out of the bottom flaps to create propellors. Cover them with foil and cross them to make an X. Fasten the propellors to the front of the plane by using an extra large paper fastener or a screw, allowing the propellors to spin.

• Cut a 15" x 15" frame out of cardboard scraps to create a windshield. Cut out an inside square to make the windshield see-through, leaving a frame two or three inches wide. Cover the empty space with clear contact paper, and tape the "window" in place.

• Create a cardboard fin to add to the back. Attach it to the box by cutting a small slit, fitting the fin through, and gluing it in place.

• Spray paint the box, then use a brush and paints to decorate it as desired. Write the words "Make a Difference in the World!" on the sides. Tie ribbons off the back end and attach ideas for ways people can get out and make a difference in the world.

• Use planes in the Promise Path Parade. Have the kids toss out small pieces of gum or candy attached to a piece of paper with a Promise Path Memory Verse.

Questions: As the children work, ask questions like these: **Where do planes take us? Why is it important to make a difference in the world? Do you know of places in the world where people have never heard about Jesus? What about places where people don't have enough food or a home to live in? What are some ways you can try to make a difference in the world?**

Kindergarten Suggestion: Younger children will need adults to help with the cutting. Another option is to pair kindergartners with fifth or sixth graders. The young children can help with wrapping the propellors and decorating the plane.

19. PROMISE PATH SCULPTURE

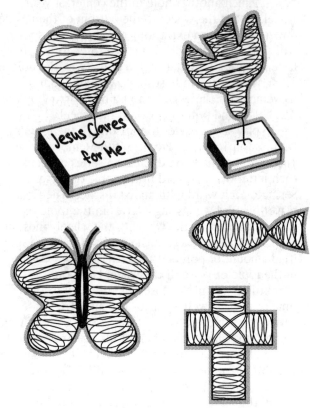

Goal: The children will make sculptures that remind them to stop and think about Jesus. This project correlates with Week 1.

Length: This project will take a minimum of two weeks to complete and is most suitable for older children (grades 3–6). It needs minimal preparation and cleanup but requires extra storage as the stain dries.

Supplies: Wood blocks (about 8" x 5"), sandpaper, pencils, permanent markers, pictures or patterns of Christian symbols (cross, fish, dove, heart, or butterfly), 14-gauge vinyl coated electrical wire, bell wire (found in hardware stores), wood stain, brushes, nails or brads, hammers

Directions:
• Sand the wood block to remove any rough edges. Use a pencil to print something special about Jesus on the wood block. Some ideas are: "Jesus Loves Me," "Jesus Died for Me," or "Jesus Cares for Me."

• Carefully trace over the pencil lines with permanent marker.

• Stain the wood as desired, using a brush to apply. Let dry until the next week.

• Have the children choose a symbol that reminds them of Jesus. Then form the 14-gauge wire into the shape of that symbol. Have one end of the wire stick out the bottom to be used to fasten to the base.

• Wrap the bell wire and coil it to fill in the shape.

• Attach the wire sculpture to the wooden block with a nail or brad.

Questions: As the children work, ask these questions or similar ones: **Why did you choose the symbol you did? How does your symbol remind you of Jesus? Why is it important to stop and think about Jesus? How will thinking about Jesus help you in your everyday life?**

Kindergarten Supplies: Sanded and stained pieces of plywood or thin boards, clear-drying glue, adhesive picture hangers
Kindergarten Suggestion: Help the little ones form their shapes—crosses and hearts would be the easiest—and fill in with wire. Glue the symbol to the wood and put a hanger on the back.

20. MAKE A DIFFERENCE GIFT CARDS

Goal: The children will make a booklet filled with service gift cards that will help make a difference in their world. This project correlates with Weeks 5 and 7.

Length: This project is a group project and will take one or two weeks to complete. It is most suitable for older children (grades 3–6). It requires minimal preparation, cleanup, and storage.

Supplies: Construction paper, velcro tape, markers, index cards, stapler. See below for more specifics.

Directions:

• Fold several sheets of construction paper in half. Use as many sheets as needed for service ideas. Staple in the center.

• Title it "Making a Difference in the World," and decorate the cover as desired.

• With the entire group, discuss a variety of service ideas that will help make a difference in the world. Write each idea down on the board so that it can be shared. Think of service ideas for the neighborhood, school, community, and world at large. Here are some ideas to get you started:

　•Assemble a church packet for new neighbors. Include brochures, newsletters, bulletins, magnets (which can be made out of card stock and magnetic tape), and an invitation to an upcoming social event at your church.

• Welcome new neighbors by giving them a small coupon book that offers older kids' services to baby-sit a child, feed a pet while they're away, rake their leaves, pull weeds, or wash their car.

• Treat your neighborhood or church community to a day of free car washes. You'll need a good group of willing volunteers, signs that say, "FREE Car Wash!" as well as buckets, soap, rags, old towels, a hose, and even a hand vacuum cleaner to give a quick fix to the car's interior.

• Treat your church community to a lawn care party. Provide needed tools and refreshments for everyone who shows up. Then mow and trim the lawn, pull weeds, plant new flowers, and spruce up areas that need a little extra care.

• Put together care kits for needy kids at the start of each school year. Check ahead of time to see which missions or service agencies in your area could distribute the kits. Ask for donations of general school supplies, or raise money to buy them. Then put together kits that include lined paper, pencils, glue, folders, pencil sharpener, erasers, markers, crayons, and spiral notebooks.

• Have a fundraising festival for your favorite cause. Do it by sponsoring a dance-a-thon or rock-a-thon (in rocking chairs), offering a community garage sale or bake sale, or by selling your favorite candy. Donate the money to an organization in need of your help.

• Write each idea on an index card. Attach a piece of velcro onto the back of each one. Center the other half of the velcro onto one sheet of construction paper.

• Pull off service project ideas as you prepare to do them. Return the card to the booklet when you are done so it can be used again.

Questions: While the children are working, ask questions such as these: **Why does God want us to make a difference in the world? How can we do that? Have you ever done something or been involved with a project that has reached out to others? How did it make you feel? How did it make them feel?**

Kindergarten Suggestion (also for first graders): Young children are eager to help others. Give them several pieces of construction paper and have them draw ways they can help others. Some ideas are: picking up litter, taking in the mail or paper for an elderly neighbor, or playing with a younger child so Mom or Dad can do something.

Grid for Project 6 (p. 89)
PROMISE PATH CHURCH CALENDAR

S	M	T	W	T	F	S

Be Quiet and Know That I Am God

Theme 1 – Based on Psalm 46:10

Words by Paula J. Bussard

Music by Ken Goodwin

When all the lights are out, and you're

Be Quiet and Know That I Am God - 2

Be Quiet and Know That I Am God - 4

Everyone Wins

Theme 2 – Based on Proverbs 12:26

Words by Paula J. Bussard

Music by Ken Goodwin

Everyone Wins - 2

Remove the Sin

Theme 3 – Based on Hebrews 12:1

Words by Paula Bussard & Roger Cadle

Music by Roger Cadle

Remove the Sin - 2

Honor Your Father and Your Mother

Theme 4 – Based on Ephesians 6:2

Words & Music by Christine Wyrtzen

Hon - or___ your fa - ther and your mo - ther.___

Let them know they're spe - cial to you___ in all you say and ev - 'ry -

Honor Your Father and Your Mother - 2

You Should Meet Together

Theme 5 – Based on Hebrews 10:25

Words by Paula Bussard

Music by Ken Goodwin

You Should Meet Together - 2

The Lord Looks at the Heart

Theme 6 – Based on 1 Samuel 16:7

Words by Paula Bussard

Music by Ken Goodwin

Look on the out - side; What do you see? I see you, and you see me.

Up - side down - side; What do you see? I see you, and you see me. But

God looks in - side. Our thoughts and feel - ings can - not __ hide. He's

there to stay. He knows what you're think-ing ev-'ry day. So

take this good ad-vice, my friend; Look at oth-ers from with-in.

Be like the good Lord from the start. See what's in their heart. The

Lord looks at the heart.

The Lord Looks at the Heart - 2

Be a Light

Theme 7 – Based on Matthew 5:16

Words by Paula J. Bussard

Music by Ken Goodwin

Show Me, O God

Theme 8 – Based on Psalm 16:11

Words by Paula Bussard

Music by Ken Goodwin

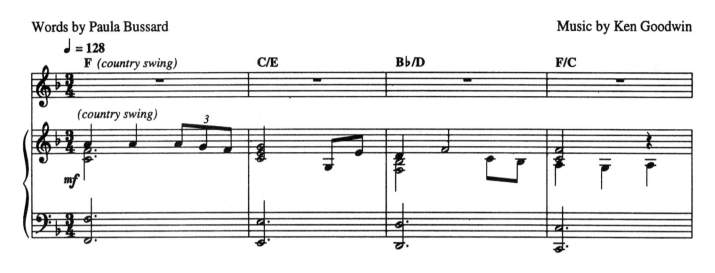

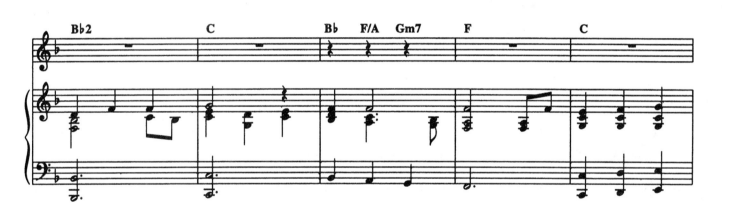

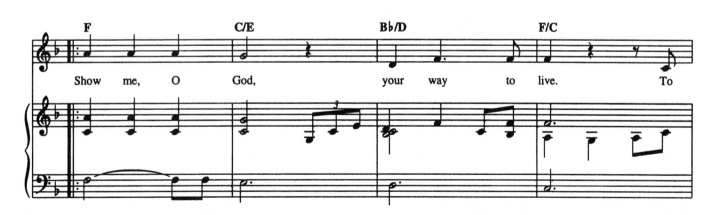

Show me, O God, your way to live. To

Show Me, O God - 2

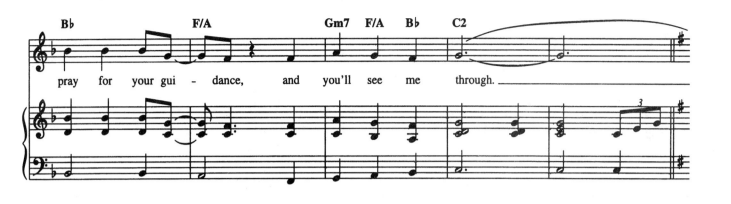

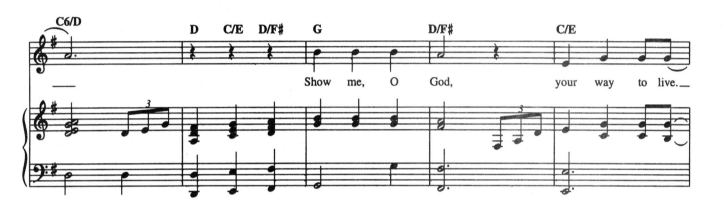

Show Me, O God - 3

Show Me, O God - 4

Photocopy and return to Mainstay Church Resources

Evaluation of the Grades 1–6 Curriculum:
Promise Kids on the Promise Path

Your feedback is important to us. Please take a few minutes to fill out this evaluation and send it to Mainstay Church Resources at the address below. We would appreciate your being as specific as possible. It might be a good idea to talk with the other adult leaders, with the children who participated, and with parents.

1. Which aspects of this curriculum did you find most helpful? What worked best with your children? Explain.

2. What did your adult leaders think about the various parts of the curriculum? How did the meeting plans work for them? Be specific.

3. How did the children respond to the program? What did they learn?

4. What suggestions do you have for improving this curriculum model for future 50-Day Adventures?

5. Was the *Promise Kids Sing-along* audiocassette helpful? If so, how?

6. Additional comments (use a separate sheet if necessary):

Name _____

Phone _____

Address _____

City _____

State/Province _____ Zip/Code _____

Church Name and City _____

PLEASE MAIL THIS EVALUATION TO:

Mainstay Church Resources
Box 30
Wheaton, Illinois 60189-0030

Photocopy and return to Mainstay Church Resources

Item	Title	Price Each	Qty	Discount Price**	Total
Promise Kids on the Promise Path					
2930	Promise Kids on the Promise Path Children's Journal (3–6)	$7.00**	_____	_____	_____
2940	Critter County® Bug Beepers for Promise Keepers Activity Book (K–2)	$7.00**	_____	_____	_____
451R	Critter County® Bug Beepers for Promise Keepers Scripture Memory Songs	$7.00**	_____	_____	_____
4515	Promise Kids Sing-along: Bible Songs for Children's Worship	$8.00	_____		_____
Other Adventures					
3805	Son Power Children's Curriculum (1–6)	$25.00	_____		_____
451L	Son Power Sing-along Children's Curriculum Bible Songs	$6.00	_____		_____
2830	Son Power for Super Kids Children's Journal (3–6)	$6.00**	_____		_____
2840	Critter County® Power Buddies Activity Book (K–2)	$6.00**	_____	_____	_____
451K	Critter County® Power Buddies Children's Stories & Bible Songs Tape	$6.00**	_____	_____	_____
3705	G.H. Construction Crew Children's Curriculum (1–6)	$25.00	_____		_____
450Z	Bible Memory Toolbox Curriculum Sing-along Songs	$6.00	_____		_____
2730	G.H. Construction Crew Children's Journal (3–6)	$6.00**	_____	_____	_____
2740	Critter County® Clubhouse Activity Book (K–2)	$6.00**	_____	_____	_____
450X	Critter County® Clubhouse Children's Scripture Memory Tape	$6.00**	_____	_____	_____
3610	Adventure Gear for God's Kids Grades 1–6 Leader's Guide & Sing-along Tape	$30.00	_____		_____
2630	Adventure Gear for God's Kids Children's Journal (3–6)	$6.00**	_____	_____	_____
2640	Pack Up My Backpack Activity Book (K–2)	$6.00**	_____	_____	_____
450S	Pack Up My Backpack Children's Scripture Memory Tape	$6.00**	_____	_____	_____

Subtotal $_____

Add 10% for UPS shipping/handling ($4.00 minimum) $_____

Canadian or Illinois residents add 7% GST/sales tax $_____

Total (subtotal + shipping + tax) $_____

Total Amount Enclosed $_____

Ship my order to:

Name _____ Phone (_____) _____

Church Name _____

Street Address* _____ City _____

State/Prov_____ Zip/Code _____

*Note: UPS will not deliver to a P.O. box.

Mail a copy of this order form with your check to:
Mainstay Church Resources, Box 30, Wheaton, IL 60189-0030
In Canada: The Chapel Ministries, Box 2000, Waterdown, ON LoR 2Ho

For VISA, MasterCard, or Discover Card orders call 1-800-224-2735 (U.S.) or 1-800-461-4114 (Canada).

**Volume purchases qualify for quantity discounts. Any combination of journals, activity books, or tapes marked with **:
10–99: $5.49; 100–299: $5.29; 300+: $5.09.

MO89CLC